Python by Example

Learning to Program in 150 Challenges

Python is today's fastest growing programming language. This engaging and refreshingly different guide breaks down the skills into clear step-by-step chunks and explains the theory using brief easy-to-understand language. Rather than bamboozling readers with pages of mind-numbing technical jargon, this book includes 150 practical challenges, putting the power in the reader's hands. Through creating programs to solve these challenges the reader will quickly progress from mastering the basics to confidently using subroutines, a graphical user interface, and linking to external text, csv and SQL files. This book is perfect for anyone who wants to learn how to program with Python. In particular, students starting out in computer science and teachers who want to improve their confidence in Python will find here a set of ready-made challenges for classroom use.

NICHOLA LACEY is Director of Nichola Wilkin Ltd. She is a trusted source for teaching resources, having sold thousands of resources to schools around the world. As one of the most popular authors on TES, Nichola enjoys an extremely high review rating with hundreds of thousands of downloads. She was a programmer before moving into corporate training and then retraining as a teacher, and she gained a unique skill set of programming and practical classroom experience after being promoted to head of computer science in a private boys' school.

PYTHON BY EXAMPLE

Learning to Program in 150 Challenges

NICHOLA LACEY
Nichola Wilkin Ltd

CAMBRIDGE
UNIVERSITY PRESS

CAMBRIDGE
UNIVERSITY PRESS

University Printing House, Cambridge CB2 8BS, United Kingdom

One Liberty Plaza, 20th Floor, New York, NY 10006, USA

477 Williamstown Road, Port Melbourne, VIC 3207, Australia

314–321, 3rd Floor, Plot 3, Splendor Forum, Jasola District Centre, New Delhi – 110025, India

103 Penang Road, #05-06/07, Visioncrest Commercial, Singapore 238467

Cambridge University Press is part of the University of Cambridge.

It furthers the University's mission by disseminating knowledge in the pursuit of education, learning, and research at the highest international levels of excellence.

www.cambridge.org
Information on this title: www.cambridge.org/9781108716833
DOI: 10.1017/9781108591942

First published 2019
5th printing 2022

Printed in Great Britain by Ashford Colour Press Ltd.

A catalogue record for this publication is available from the British Library.

ISBN 978-1-108-71683-3 Paperback

Contents

Image Credits

Animal Drawings:

Introduction

 If you have ever picked up a programming manual and felt your forehead go clammy and your eyes cross as you attempt to make sense of the long-winded explanations, this is the guide for you.

I have been in your position, attempting to learn how to program and having to rely on the traditional style of guides. I know from painful experience how quickly I glaze over and my brain solidifies; after only a few pages the tedium leaves me blindly reading words without any real notion of what they mean any more. Inevitably I give up and the whole process makes me feel like a limp failure, gasping for breath after I surface from drowning in technical jargon.

I hated having to read through pointless drivel and then be presented with a short program telling me exactly what to type in and then spend the next 20 pages reading about what I have just done and the 101 ways I could run it. I hated having no control over trying things out for myself and I hated the way these guides would only contain one or two challenges at the end of a chapter of theory.

I knew there had to be a better way, and thankfully there is. I wrote it and you are presently reading it, so aren't you lucky? This guide is refreshingly different and helps you learn how to program with Python by using practical examples rather than self-important explanations.

Many programmers learn through experimentation, looking at others' code and working out what method is best for a given situation. This book is a hands-on approach to learning programming. After minimal reading you are set a number of challenges to create the programs. You can explore and experiment with the programming language and look at the example solutions to learn how to think like a programmer. There are no chapters entitled "the architecture of a computer", "the theory of programming" or any other gobbledy-gook other authors like to waste time with. I don't want to baffle you with theory or blind you with overbearing explanations that suck out your enthusiasm for learning to program.

Hopefully, you want to get stuck into creating programs, solving problems and enjoying the sense of accomplishment that you get as you proudly look over your lines of code, knowing that you created something that works. That is great, your eagerness is to be applauded and I salute those who are reading this while already sitting at their computers, fingers poised and ready to get going. If that is the case, that you already have Python open on your screen and are itching to get going, then away you go and I'll see you in the first chapter called "The Basics" on page 11.

For everyone who is still with us and is feeling a little more timid, there are just a few more things to tell you about before you take the plunge.

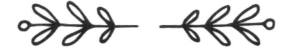

How to Use This Book

This book builds from very simple programs to more complex ones. If you are new to programming or new to Python, start with "The Basics" and work through the chapters in order.

If you are familiar with Python programming and feel confident with the basics, the theory and logic surrounding programming, then you can just dip in and out of the book to get help on the specifics you need.

The book is split into two sections:

Part I

In Part I, each chapter takes you through some basic programming rules and challenges for you to complete and includes:

- a **simple explanation** giving you pointers, which is useful if you are new to programming in Python;

- **examples of code** with a short explanation, which you can use as a basis to solve the challenges;

- a **list of challenges** for you to work through that get harder as you move through them. Each challenge should only take between a couple of minutes and 20 minutes to solve; however, some of the more complex challenges near the end of Part I will take longer as you build up the techniques you will be using. Don't panic if you take longer than this, as long as you solve the problems without *too* much copying from the suggested solution, you are doing fine;

- code containing a **possible solution** for each challenge; there is often more than one answer available, but we include just a single program as a possible solution that you can refer to if you get stuck on a particular aspect of the code.

Part II

In Part II, you are given some larger challenges which utilize the programming skills you learnt in Part I and allow you to consolidate and reinforce the techniques you have been practising. In this section, you are not given the help and example code that is given in Part I and it will take longer to solve each challenge. After each challenge, you are given one possible answer that you may find useful if you are stuck. However, you may have found another solution that works just as well.

Who Is This Book For?

This book is suitable for anyone who wants to learn how to program with Python. It is an essential tool for teachers and students in Key Stage 3 or those studying computer science who need help and ready-made examples to practise programming techniques and build confidence. It can also be used to help with a computer science programming project resource bank, to help pupils needing additional support or just a quick reminder of the syntax when creating programs.

Downloading Python

You can download Python for free from the official Python website:

www.python.org/downloads/

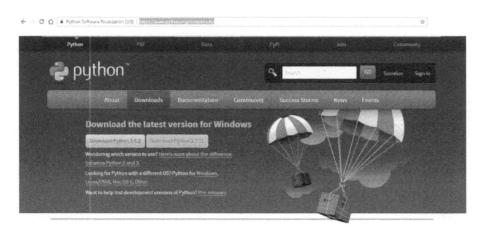

Click on the latest version (in the example above, click on the **Download Python 3.6.2** button) to start the installation.

The program will download an executable (.exe) file. When you run this program, you will see an install window like the one shown below.

Click the **Install Now** option and the program will start installing Python onto your system.

Running Python

To start Python on a Windows system, click on the **Windows** icon or **Start** menu and select the **IDLE (Python version number)** option as highlighted below.

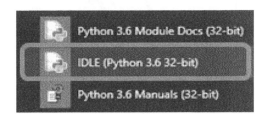

Python 3.6 Module Docs (32-bit)

IDLE (Python 3.6 32-bit)

Python 3.6 Manuals (32-bit)

Some Tips

File Location

On a Windows system, the Python folder is usually found in the C:\ drive and will be named **Python36** (or similar) and the files will automatically be saved in the same location, unless you save them specifically in another location.

Using Comments

Comments are a very useful tool for programmers. They serve two purposes:

- adding an explanation of how the program works;

- stopping parts of the program from working temporarily so you can run and test other parts of the program.

The first, and original, purpose of explaining how a program works is so other programmers can make sense of your programs in case your code needs to be altered and updated in the future and to remind you about why you wrote particular lines of code.

```
print("This is a simple program")
print() #Outputs a blank line to help with layout
name = input("Please input your name: ")#Asks for an input
print("Hello", name) #Joins "Hello" and their name together
```

In this example, comments have been added at the end of the last three lines. They are shown in red and start with the # symbol.

In reality, you would not add comments on lines which contain obvious code as it would clutter the screen; you would only add comments where necessary.

As Python knows to ignore anything after a # symbol, programmers soon started to use # at the start of lines of their code to block out sections they do not want to run so they can focus on and test others.

```
#print("This is a simple program")
print()
name = input("Please input your name: ")
print("Hello", name)
```

In this example, the # has been added to the first line of the program to temporarily stop it from running. To bring it back into the running order simply delete the # and the code will be reactivated.

In this guide, we have not included any comments to the programs so you have to read the code to make sense of it. That way you will really learn how to code! If you are creating programs as part of your coursework you should add comments to explain your programming to the examiner.

Formatting Python

In most versions of Python IDLE it is possible to quickly add comments and indent code using the menus. This way, if you need to block out entire areas using a comment you simply highlight the lines and then select the **Format** menu and select **Comment Out Region**. Similarly, if you need to indent a region (we will look at the reason for indenting code later) then you can also easily do this with the menu.

File	Edit	Format	Run	Options	Windows	Help

Indent Region	Ctrl+]
Dedent Region	Ctrl+[
Comment Out Region	Alt+3
Uncomment Region	Alt+4

Okay, that is all the "housekeeping" out of the way. No more procrastinating; take a deep breath and away we go...

Part 1

Learning Python

The Basics

Explanation

This is the **shell** window and is the first screen you see when you launch Python.

```
Python 3.6.3 Shell
File  Edit  Shell  Debug  Options  Window  Help
Python 3.6.3 (v3.6.3:2c5fed8, Oct  3 2017, 17:26:49) [MSC v.1900 32 bit (Intel)] on win32
Type "copyright", "credits" or "license()" for more information.
>>> |
```

It is possible to write Python code straight into the shell, but as soon as you hit [Return] at the end of a line, it will run that line of code. This may be suitable for using Python as a quick calculator; for instance, you can type in **3*5** at the prompt and Python will show the answer **15** on the next line; however, this style of inputting is not useful for more complex programs.

It is much better to start a new window, create all the code in the new window, save your code and run it.

To create a new window in which to write your code, select **File** and **New**. Once you enter your code in this new window you can save it and run it all in one go. This will then run the code in the shell window.

Alternatively, Python programs can be written using any text editor and must be saved with the file name extension .py in order to work. These programs can then be run from the command prompt by typing in the full directory root and file name.

Running Your Program

Every time you run the code your program will need to be saved afresh in case there have been any changes to it.

In this version of Python, you can run the program by selecting the **Run** menu and selecting **Run Module**. Alternatively, you can press the **[F5]** key. If this is the first time the program is saved, Python will prompt you to name and save the file before it will allow the program to run.

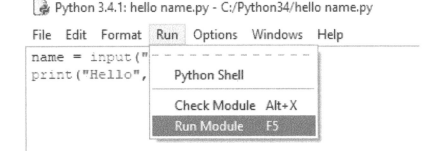

Important Things to Note When Writing Your Programs

Python is case sensitive so it is important that you use the correct case, otherwise your code <u>will not work</u>.

Text values need to appear in speech marks (") but numbers do not.

When naming **variables** (i.e. values that you want to store data in) you cannot use any dedicated words such as print, input, etc. otherwise your code will not work.

When saving your files **do not save them with any dedicated words** that Python already uses, such as print, input, etc. If you do this it will not run and you will need to rename the file before it works.

To edit a program you have saved and closed, right-click on the file and select **Edit with IDLE**. If you just double-click on the file it will only try to run it and you will not be able to edit it.

Example Code

```
num1 = 93
```
Set the value of a **variable**, if there is not a variable already created, it will create one. A variable is a container for a value (in this case the variable will be called "num1" and store the value 93). The value stored in the variable can change while the program is running. The variable can be called whatever you want (except Python dedicated words such as print, save, etc.) and it must start with a letter rather than a number or symbol and have no spaces.

```
answer = num1 + num2
```
Adds together num1 and num2 and stores the answer in a variable called answer.

```
answer = num1 - num2
```
Subtracts num2 from num1 and stores the answer in a variable called answer.

```
answer = num1 * num2
```
Multiplies num1 by num2 and stores the answer in a variable called answer.

```
answer = num1 / num2
```
Divides num1 by num2 and stores the answer in a variable called answer.

```
answer = num1 // num2
```
A whole number division (i.e. 9//4 = 2) and stores the answer in a variable called answer.

```
print ("This is a message")
```
Displays the message in the brackets. As the value we want displayed is a text value it has the speech marks, which will not be displayed in the output. If you wanted to display a numerical value or the contents of a variable, the speech marks are not needed.

```
print ("First line\nSecond line")
```
"\n" is used as a line break.

```
print ("The answer is", answer)
```
Displays the text "The answer is" and the value of the variable answer.

```
textValue = input("Enter a text value: ")
```
Displays the question "Enter a text value: " and stores the value the user enters in a variable called textValue. The space after the colon allows a space to be added before the user enters their answer, otherwise they appear squashed unattractively together.

```
numValue = int(input("Enter a number: "))
```
Displays the question "Enter a number: " and stores the value as an integer (a whole number) in a variable called numValue Integers can be used in calculations but variables stored as text cannot.

Challenges

001

Ask for the user's first name and display the output message **Hello [First Name]**.

002

Ask for the user's first name and then ask for their surname and display the output message **Hello [First Name] [Surname]**.

003

Write code that will display the joke "What do you call a bear with no teeth?" and on the next line display the answer "A gummy bear!" Try to create it using only one line of code.

004

Ask the user to enter two numbers. Add them together and display the answer as **The total is [answer]**.

005

Ask the user to enter three numbers. Add together the first two numbers and then multiply this total by the third. Display the answer as **The answer is [answer]**.

006

Ask how many slices of pizza the user started with and ask how many slices they have eaten. Work out how many slices they have left and display the answer in a user-friendly format.

007

Ask the user for their name and their age. Add 1 to their age and display the output **[Name] next birthday you will be [new age]**.

008

Ask for the total price of the bill, then ask how many diners there are. Divide the total bill by the number of diners and show how much each person must pay.

009

Write a program that will ask for a number of days and then will show how many hours, minutes and seconds are in that number of days.

010

There are 2,204 pounds in a kilogram. Ask the user to enter a weight in kilograms and convert it to pounds.

Keep going, you are doing well.

011

Task the user to enter a number over 100 and then enter a number under 10 and tell them how many times the smaller number goes into the larger number in a user-friendly format.

Answers

001

```
firstname = input("Please enter your first name: ")
print ("Hello",firstname)
```

002

```
firstname = input("Please enter your first name: ")
surname = input("Please enter your surname: ")
print ("Hello",firstname, surname)
```

003

```
print("What do you call a bear with no teeth?\nA gummy bear!")
```

004

```
num1 = int(input("Please enter your first number: "))
num2 = int(input("Please enter your second number: "))
answer = num1 + num2
print("The answer is", answer)
```

005

```
num1 = int(input("Please enter your first number: "))
num2 = int(input("Please enter your second number: "))
num3 = int(input("Please enter your third number: "))
answer = (num1 + num2)* num3
print("The answer is", answer)
```

006

```
startNum = int(input("Enter the number of slices of pizza you started with: "))
endNum = int(input("How many slices have you eaten? "))
slicesLeft = startNum - endNum
print("You have", slicesLeft, "slices remaining")
```

007

```
name = input("What is your name? ")
age = int(input("How old are you? "))
newAge = age + 1
print(name, "next birthday you will be", newAge)
```

008

```
bill = int(input("What is the total cost of the bill? "))
people = int(input("How many people are there? "))
each = bill/people
print("Each person should pay £", each)
```

009

```
days = int(input("Enter the number of days: "))
hours = days*24
minutes = hours*60
seconds = minutes*60
print("In", days,"days there are...")
print(hours, "hours")
print(minutes, "minutes")
print(seconds, "seconds")
```

010

```
kilo = int(input("Enter the number of kilos: "))
pound = kilo * 2.204
print("That is", pound,"pounds")
```

011

```
larger = int(input("Enter a number over 100: "))
smaller = int(input("Enter a number under 10: "))
answer = larger//smaller
print(smaller,"goes into", larger, answer,"times")
```

How did you do? Don't forget, the skills you are learning now will help you later.

If Statements

Explanation

If statements allow your program to make a decision and change the route that is taken through the program.

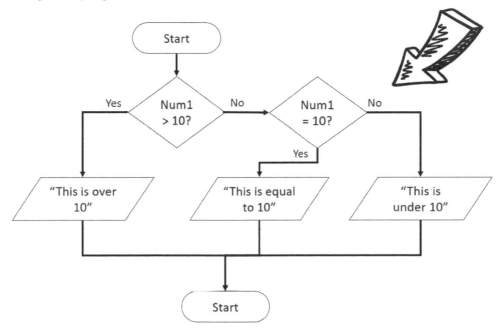

Below is how the if statement for this flow chart would look in Python.

```python
if num1 > 10:
    print("This is over 10")
elif num1 == 10:
    print("This is equal to 10")
else:
    print("This is under 10")
```

Indenting Lines of Code

Indenting is very important in Python as it shows the lines that are dependent on others, as shown in the example on the previous page. In order to indent text you can use your [**Tab**] key or you can press your [**space key**] five times. The [**backspace**] key will remove indents.

The first line of the if statement tests a condition, and if that condition is met (i.e. the first condition is true) then the lines of code directly below it are run. If it is not met (i.e. the first condition is false) it will test the second condition, if there is one, and so on. Below are examples of the different comparison and logical operators you can use in the condition line of your if statement.

Comparison Operators

Operator	Description
==	Equal to
!=	Not equal to
>	Greater than
<	Less than
>=	Greater than or equal to
<=	Less than or equal to

Logical Operators

Operator	Description
and	Both conditions must be met
or	Either condition must be met

Example Code

Please note: In the examples shown, num is a variable entered by the user that has been stored as an integer.

```
if num > 10:
 print("This is over 10")
else:
 print("This is not over 10")
```
If num1 is over 10, it will display the message "This is over 10", otherwise it will display the message "This is under 10".

```
if num > 10:
 print("This is over 10")
elif num == 10:
 print("This is equal to 10")
else:
 print("This is under 10")
```
If num1 is over 10, it will display the message "This is over 10", otherwise it will check the next condition. If num1 is equal to 10, it will display the message "This is equal to 10". Otherwise, if neither of the first two conditions have been met, it will display the message "This is under 10".

```
if num >= 10:
 if num <= 20:
  print("This is between 10 and 20")
 else:
  print("This is over 20")
else:
 print("This is under 10")
```
If num1 is 10 or more then it will test another if statement to see if num1 is less than or equal to 20. If it is, it will display the message "This is between 10 and 20". If num1 is not less than or equal to 20 then it will display the message "This is over 20". If num1 is not over 10, it will display the message "This is under 10".

```
text = str.lower(text)
```
Changes the text to lower case. As Python is case sensitive, this changes the data input by the user into lower case so it is easier to check.

```
num = int(input("Enter a number between 10 and 20: "))
if num >= 10 and num <= 20:
 print("Thank you")
else:
 print("Out of range")
```

This uses **and** to test multiple conditions in the if statement. Both the conditions must be met to produce the output "Thank you".

```
num = int(input("Enter an EVEN number between 1 and 5: "))
if num == 2 or num == 4:
 print("Thank you")
else:
 print("Incorrect")
```

This uses **or** to test the conditions in the if statement. Just one condition must be met to display the output "Thank you".

Challenges

012
Ask for two numbers. If the first one is larger than the second, display the second number first and then the first number, otherwise show the first number first and then the second.

013
Ask the user to enter a number that is under 20. If they enter a number that is 20 or more, display the message "Too high", otherwise display "Thank you".

014
Ask the user to enter a number between 10 and 20 (inclusive). If they enter a number within this range, display the message "Thank you", otherwise display the message "Incorrect answer".

015
Ask the user to enter their favourite colour. If they enter "red", "RED" or "Red" display the message "I like red too", otherwise display the message "I don't like [colour], I prefer red".

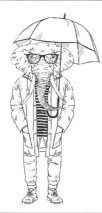

016
Ask the user if it is raining and convert their answer to lower case so it doesn't matter what case they type it in. If they answer "yes", ask if it is windy. If they answer "yes" to this second question, display the answer "It is too windy for an umbrella", otherwise display the message "Take an umbrella". If they did not answer yes to the first question, display the answer "Enjoy your day".

017
Ask the user's age. If they are 18 or over, display the message "You can vote", if they are aged 17, display the message "You can learn to drive", if they are 16, display the message "You can buy a lottery ticket", if they are under 16, display the message "You can go Trick-or-Treating".

018
Ask the user to enter a number. If it is under 10, display the message "Too low", if their number is between 10 and 20, display "Correct", otherwise display "Too high".

019
Ask the user to enter 1, 2 or 3. If they enter a 1, display the message "Thank you", if they enter a 2, display "Well done", if they enter a 3, display "Correct". If they enter anything else, display "Error message".

Answers

012

```
num1 = int(input("Enter first number: "))
num2 = int(input("Enter second number: "))
if num1 > num2:
    print(num2, num1)
else:
    print(num1,num2)
```

013

```
num = int(input("Enter a value less than 20: "))
if num >= 20:
    print("Too high")
else:
    print("Thank you")
```

014

```
num = int(input("Enter a value between 10 and 20: "))
if num >= 10 and num <= 20:
    print("Thank you")
else:
    print("Incorrect answer")
```

015

```
colour = input("Type in your favourite colour: ")
if colour == "red" or colour == "RED" or colour == "Red":
    print("I like red too.")
else:
    print("I don't like that colour, I prefer red")
```

016

```python
raining = input("Is it raining? ")
raining = str.lower(raining)
if raining == "yes":
    windy = input("Is it windy? ")
    windy = str.lower(windy)
    if windy == "yes":
        print("It is too windy for an umberella")
    else:
        print("Take an umberella")
else:
    print("Enjoy your day")
```

017

```python
age = int(input("What is your age? "))
if age >= 18:
    print ("You can vote")
elif age == 17:
    print ("You can learn to drive")
elif age == 16:
    print ("You can buy a lottery ticket")
else:
    print ("You can go Trick-or-Treating")
```

018

```python
num = int(input("Enter a number: "))
if num <10:
    print("Too low")
elif num >=10 and num <=20:
    print("Correct")
else:
    print("Too high")
```

019

```python
num = input("Enter 1, 2 or 3: ")
if num == "1":
    print("Thank you")
elif num == "2":
    print("Well done")
elif num == "3":
    print("Correct")
else:
    print("Error message")
```

Strings

Explanation

String is the technical name for text. To define a block of code as a string, you need to include it in either double quotes (") or single quotes ('). It doesn't matter which you use so long as you are consistent.

There are some characters you need to be particularly careful with when inputting them into strings. These include:

" ' \

That is because these symbols have special meanings in Python and it can get confusing if you use them in a string.

If you want to use one of these symbols you need to precede it with a backslash symbol and then Python will know to ignore the symbol and will treat it as normal text that is to be displayed.

Symbol	How to type this into a Python string
"	\"
'	\'
\	\\

Strings and Numbers as Variables

If you define a variable as a string, even if it only contains numbers, you cannot later use that string as part of a calculation. If you want to use a variable that has been defined as a string in a calculation, you will have to convert the string to a number before it can be used.

```
num = input("Enter a number: ")
total = num + 10
print(total)
```

In this example, the author has asked for a number, but has not defined it as a numeric value and when the program is run they will get the following error:

```
Enter a number: 45
Traceback (most recent call last):
  File "C:/Python34/CHALLENGES/String/example.py", line 2, in <module>
    total = num + 10
TypeError: Can't convert 'int' object to str implicitly
>>>
```

Although this error message looks scary, it is simply saying that the line **total = num + 10** isn't working as the variable num is defined as a string.

This problem can be solved in one of two ways. You can either define it as a number when the variable is being originally created, using this line:

```
num = int(input("Enter a number: "))
```

or you can convert it to a number after it has been created using this line:

```
num = int(num)
```

The same can happen with strings.

```
name = input("Enter a name: ")
num = int(input("Enter a number: "))
ID = name + num
print(ID)
```

In this program, the user is asked to enter their name and a number. They want it joined together and with strings the addition symbol is used as **concatenation**. When this code is run you will get a similar error message to before:

```
Enter a name: Bob
Enter a number: 23
Traceback (most recent call last):
  File "C:/Python34/CHALLENGES/String/example.py", line 3, in <module>
    ID = name + num
TypeError: Can't convert 'int' object to str implicitly
>>>
```

To get around this, either don't define the variable as a number in the first place or convert it to a string afterwards using the line:

$$num = str(num)$$

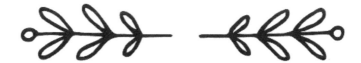

Multiple-Line Strings

If you want to input a string across multiple lines you can either use the line break (**\n**) or you can enclose the entire thing in triple quotes. This will preserve the formatting of the text.

```
address="""123 Long Lane
Oldtown
AB1 23CD"""
print(address)
```

Example Code

Please note: In the following examples, the terms word, phrase, name, firstname and surname are all variable names.

```
len(word)
```
Finds the length of the variable called word.

```
print(word.capitalize())
```
Displays the variable so only the first word has a capital letter at the beginning and everything else is in lower case.

```
name = firstname+surname
```
Joins the first name and surname together without a space between them, known as concatenation

```
word.upper()
```
Changes the string into upper case.

```
word.lower()
```
Changes the string into lower case.

```
word.title()
```
Changes a phrase so that every word has a capital letter at the beginning with the rest of the letters in the word in lower case (i.e. Title Case).

```
text = " This is some text. "
print(text.strip(" "))
```
Removes extra characters (in this case spaces) from the start and end of a string.

```
print ("Hello world"[7:10])
```
Each letter is assigned an index number to identify its position in the phrase, including the space. Python starts counting from 0, not 1.

0	1	2	3	4	5	6	7	8	9	10
H	e	l	l	o		w	o	r	l	d

Therefore, in this example, it would display the value of positions 7, 8 and 9 ,which is "orl".

Don't forget that you can reuse previous programs to save time when you are making new programs. Simply use SAVE AS and give it a new name.

Challenges

020

Ask the user to enter their first name and then display the length of their name.

021

Ask the user to enter their first name and then ask them to enter their surname. Join them together with a space between and display the name and the length of whole name.

022

Ask the user to enter their first name and surname in lower case. Change the case to title case and join them together. Display the finished result.

023

Ask the user to type in the first line of a nursery rhyme and display the length of the string. Ask for a starting number and an ending number and then display just that section of the text (remember Python starts counting from 0 and not 1).

024

Ask the user to type in any word and display it in upper case.

025

Ask the user to enter their first name. If the length of their first name is under five characters, ask them to enter their surname and join them together (without a space) and display the name in upper case. If the length of the first name is five or more characters, display their first name in lower case.

Don't forget, you can always look back, remind yourself of some of the earlier skills you have learnt. You have learnt a great deal so far.

026

Pig Latin takes the first consonant of a word, moves it to the end of the word and adds on an "ay". If a word begins with a vowel you just add "way" to the end. For example, pig becomes igpay, banana becomes ananabay, and aadvark becomes aadvarkway. Create a program that will ask the user to enter a word and change it into Pig Latin. Make sure the new word is displayed in lower case.

Answers

020

```python
name = input("Enter your first name: ")
length = len(name)
print(length)
```

021

```python
firstname = input("Enter your first name: ")
surname = input("Enter your surname: ")
name = firstname + " " + surname
length = len(name)
print(name)
print(length)
```

022

```python
firstname = input("Enter your first name in lowercase: " )
surname = input("Enter your surname in lowercase: " )
firstname = firstname.title()
surname = surname.title()
name = firstname + " " + surname
print(name)
```

023

```python
phrase = input("Enter the first line of a nursery rhyme: ")
length = len(phrase)
print("This has", length, "letters in it")
start = int(input("Enter a starting number: "))
end = int(input("Enter an end number: "))
part = (phrase[start:end])
print(part)
```

024

```python
word = input("Enter a word: ")
word = word.upper()
print(word)
```

025

```
name = input("Enter your first name: ")
if len(name)< 5:
    surname = input("Enter your surname: ")
    name = name+surname
    print(name.upper())
else:
    print(name.lower())
```

026

```
word = input("Please enter a word: ")
first = word[0]
length = len(word)
rest = word[1:length]
if first != "a" and first != "e" and first != "i" and first != "o" and first != "u":
    newword = rest + first + "ay"
else:
    newword = word + "way"
print(newword.lower())
```

Maths

Explanation

Python can perform several mathematical functions, but these are only available when the data is treated as either an **integer** (a whole number) or a **floating-point** (a number with a decimal place). If data is stored as a string, even if it only contains numeric characters, Python is unable to perform calculations with it (see page 24 for a fuller explanation).

Example Code

Please note: In order to use some of the mathematical functions (`math.sqrt(num)` and `math.pi`) you will need to import the maths library at the start of your program. You do this by typing **import math** as the first line of your program.

```
print(round(num,2))
```
Displays a number rounded to two decimal places.

```
**
```
To the power of (e.g. 10² is 10**2).

```
math.sqrt(num)
```
The square root of a number, but you must have the line **import math** at the top of your program for this to work.

```
num=float(input("Enter number: "))
```
Allows numbers with a decimal point dividing the integer and fraction part.

```
math.pi
```
Gives you pi (π) to 15 decimal places, but you must have the line **import math** at the top of your program for this to work.

```
x // y
```
Whole number division (e.g.15//2 gives the answer 7).

```
x % y
```
Finds the remainder (e.g. 15%2 gives the answer 1).

Challenges

027
Ask the user to enter a number with lots of decimal places. Multiply this number by two and display the answer.

028
Update program 027 so that it will display the answer to two decimal places.

029
Ask the user to enter an integer that is over 500. Work out the square root of that number and display it to two decimal places.

030
Display pi (π) to five decimal places.

031
Ask the user to enter the radius of a circle (measurement from the centre point to the edge). Work out the area of the circle (π*radius²).

032
Ask for the radius and the depth of a cylinder and work out the total volume (circle area*depth) rounded to three decimal places.

033
Ask the user to enter two numbers. Use whole number division to divide the first number by the second and also work out the remainder and display the answer in a user-friendly way (e.g. if they enter 7 and 2 display "7 divided by 2 is 3 with 1 remaining").

034
Display the following message:
```
        1) Square
        2) Triangle

    Enter a number:
```
If the user enters 1, then it should ask them for the length of one of its sides and display the area. If they select 2, it should ask for the base and height of the triangle and display the area. If they type in anything else, it should give them a suitable error message.

You are starting to think like a programmer.

Answers

027

```
num = float(input("Enter a number with lots of decimal places: "))
print(num*2)
```

028

```
num = float(input("Enter a number with lots of decimal places: "))
answer = num*2
print(answer)
print (round(answer, 2))
```

029

```
import math
num = int(input("Enter a number over 500: "))
answer = math.sqrt(num)
print (round(answer, 2))
```

030

```
import math
print(round(math.pi,5))
```

031

```
import math
radius = int(input("Enter the radius of the circle: "))
area = math.pi*(radius**2)
print(area)
```

032

```
import math
radius = int(input("Enter the radius of the circle: "))
depth = int(input("Enter depth: "))
area = math.pi*(radius**2)
volume = area*depth
print(round(volume,3))
```

033

```
num1=int(input("Enter a number: "))
num2=int(input("Enter another number: "))
ans1 = num1//num2
ans2 = num1%num2
print(num1, "divided by", num2, "is", ans1, "with", ans2, "remaining.")
```

034

```python
print("1) Square")
print("2) Triangle")
print()
menuselection = int(input("Enter a number: "))
if menuselection == 1:
    side = int(input("Enter the length of one side: "))
    area = side*side
    print("The area of your chosen shape is", area)
elif menuselection == 2:
    base = int(input("Enter the length of the base: "))
    height = int(input("Enter the height of the triangle: "))
    area = (base*height)/2
    print("The area of your chosen shape is", area)
else:
    print("Incorrect option selected")
```

For Loop

Explanation

A **for loop** allows Python to keep repeating code a set number of times. It is sometimes known as a **counting loop** because you know the number of times the loop will run before it starts.

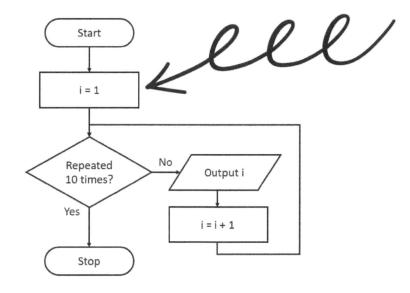

In this case, it starts at 1 and will keep repeating the loop (displaying i) until it reaches 10 and then stops. This is how this loop would look in Python

```
for i in range(1,10):
    print(i)
```

In this example, the outputs would be 1, 2, 3, 4, 5, 6, 7, 8 and 9. **When it gets to 10 the loop would stop so 10 would not be shown in the output.**

Remember to indent the lines of code within the for loop.

Example Code

The range function is often used in for loops and lists the starting number, the ending number and can also include the steps (e.g. counting in 1s, 5s or any other value you wish).

```
for i in range(1,10):
 print(i)
```
This loop uses a variable called "i" to keep track of the number of times the loop has been repeated. It will start i at 1 (as that is the starting value in the range function) and repeat the loop, adding 1 to i each time and displaying the value of i until it reaches 10 (as dictated by the range function), where it will stop. Therefore, it will not repeat the loop a tenth time and will only have the following output:

1, 2, 3, 4, 5, 6, 7, 8, 9

```
for i in range(1,10,2):
 print(i)
```
This range function includes a third value which shows how much is added to i in each loop (in this case 2). The output will therefore be: **1, 3, 5, 7, 9**

```
for i in range(10,1,-3):
 print(i)
```
This range will subtract 3 from i each time. The output will be: **10, 7, 4**

Using loops is a powerful programming tool that you will use a lot in the more challenging programs.

```
for i in word:
 print(i)
```
This would display each character in a string called "word" as a separate output (i.e. on a separate line).

Challenges

035
Ask the user to enter their name and then display their name three times.

036
Alter program 035 so that it will ask the user to enter their name and a number and then display their name that number of times.

037
Ask the user to enter their name and display each letter in their name on a separate line.

038
Change program 037 to also ask for a number. Display their name (one letter at a time on each line) and repeat this for the number of times they entered.

039
Ask the user to enter a number between 1 and 12 and then display the times table for that number.

040

Ask for a number below 50 and then count down from 50 to that number, making sure you show the number they entered in the output.

041
Ask the user to enter their name and a number. If the number is less than 10, then display their name that number of times; otherwise display the message "Too high" three times.

042
Set a variable called total to 0. Ask the user to enter five numbers and after each input ask them if they want that number included. If they do, then add the number to the total. If they do not want it included, don't add it to the total. After they have entered all five numbers, display the total.

043
Ask which direction the user wants to count (up or down). If they select up, then ask them for the top number and then count from 1 to that number. If they select down, ask them to enter a number below 20 and then count down from 20 to that number. If they entered something other than up or down, display the message "I don't understand".

044
Ask how many people the user wants to invite to a party. If they enter a number below 10, ask for the names and after each name display "[name] has been invited". If they enter a number which is 10 or higher, display the message "Too many people".

Answers

035

```
name = input("Type in your name: ")
for i in range (0,3):
    print(name)
```

036

```
name = input("Type in your name: ")
number = int(input("Enter a number: "))
for i in range (0,number):
    print(name)
```

037

```
name = input("Enter your name: ")
for i in name:
    print(i)
```

038

```
num = int(input("Enter a number: "))
name = input("Enter your name: ")
for x in range(0,num):
    for i in name:
        print(i)
```

039

```
num = int(input("Enter a number between 1 and 12: "))
for i in range(1, 13):
    answer = i * num
    print (i, "x", num, "=", answer)
```

040

```
num = int(input("Enter a number below 50: "))
for i in range(50,num-1, -1):
    print(i)
```

041

```
name = input("Enter your name: ")
num = int(input("Enter a number: "))
if num < 10:
    for i in range(0,num):
        print(name)
else:
    for i in range(0,3):
        print("Too high")
```

042

```
total = 0
for i in range(0,5):
    num = int(input("Enter a number: "))
    ans = input("Do you want this number included? (y/n) ")
    if ans == "y":
        total = total + num
print(total)
```

043

```
direction = input("Do you want to count up or down? (u/d) ")
if direction == "u":
    num = int(input("What is the top number? "))
    for i in range(1,num+1):
        print(i)
elif direction == "d":
    num = int(input("Enter a number below 20: "))
    for i in range(20,num-1, -1):
        print(i)
else:
    print("I don't understand")
```

044

```
num = int(input("How many friends do you want to invite to the party? "))
if num < 10:
    for i in range(0,num):
        name = input("Enter a name: ")
        print(name, "has been invited")
else:
    print("Too many people")
```

While Loop

Explanation

A **while loop** allows code to be repeated an unknown number of times as long as a condition is being met. This may be 100 times, just the once or even never. In a while loop the condition is checked before the code is run, which means it could skip the loop altogether if the condition is not being met to start with. It is important, therefore, to make sure the correct conditions are in place to run the loop before it starts.

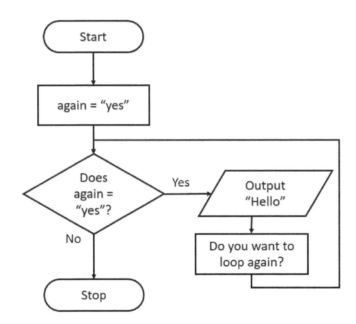

In Python the example for the flow chart above would look as follows:

```python
again = "yes"
while again == "yes":
    print ("Hello")
    again=input("Do you want to loop again? ")
```

It will keep repeating this code until the user enters anything other than "yes".

Example Code

```
total = 0
while total < 100:
 num = int(input("Enter a number: "))
 total = total + num
print("The total is", total)
```

The above program will create a variable called total and store the value as 0. It will ask the user to enter a number and will add it to the total. It will keep repeating this as long as the total is still below 100. When the total equals 100 or more, it will stop running the loop and display the total.

Comparison Operators

Operator	Description
==	Equal to
!=	Not equal to
>	Greater than
<	Less than
>=	Greater than or equal to
<=	Less than or equal to

Logical Operators

Operator	Description
and	Both conditions must be met
or	Either condition must be met

Remember: text values must appear in speech marks and numeric values do not.

Challenges

045

Set the total to 0 to start with. While the total is 50 or less, ask the user to input a number. Add that number to the total and print the message "The total is… [total]". Stop the loop when the total is *over 50.*

046

Ask the user to enter a number. Keep asking until they enter a value *over 5* and then display the message "The last number you entered was a [number]" and stop the program.

047

Ask the user to enter a number and then enter another number. Add these two numbers together and then ask if they want to add another number. If they enter "y", ask them to enter another number and keep adding numbers until they do not answer "y". Once the loop has stopped, display the total.

048

Ask for the name of somebody the user wants to invite to a party. After this, display the message "[name] has now been invited" and add 1 to the count. Then ask if they want to invite somebody else. Keep repeating this until they no longer want to invite anyone else to the party and then display how many people they have coming to the party.

049

Create a variable called compnum and set the value to 50. Ask the user to enter a number. While their guess is not the same as the compnum value, tell them if their guess is too low or too high and ask them to have another guess. If they enter the same value as compnum, display the message "Well done, you took [count] attempts".

050

Ask the user to enter a number between 10 and 20. If they enter a value under 10, display the message "Too low" and ask them to try again. If they enter a value above 20, display the message "Too high" and ask them to try again. Keep repeating this until they enter a value that is between 10 and 20 and then display the message "Thank you".

051

Using the song "10 green bottles", display the lines "There are [num] green bottles hanging on the wall, [num] green bottles hanging on the wall, and if 1 green bottle should accidentally fall". Then ask the question "how many green bottles will be hanging on the wall?" If the user answers correctly, display the message "There will be [num] green bottles hanging on the wall". If they answer incorrectly, display the message "No, try again" until they get it right. When the number of green bottles gets down to 0, display the message "There are no more green bottles hanging on the wall".

Answers

045

```python
total = 0
while total <= 50:
    num = int(input("Enter a number: "))
    total = total + num
    print("The total is...",total)
```

046

```python
num = 0
while num <= 5:
    num = int(input("Enter a number: "))
print("The last number you entered was a", num)
```

047

```python
num1 = int(input("Enter a number: "))
total = num1
again = "y"
while again == "y":
    num2 = int(input("Enter another number: "))
    total = total + num2
    again = input("Do you want to add another number? (y/n) ")
print("The total is ",total)
```

048

```python
again = "y"
count = 0
while again =="y":
    name = input("Enter a name of sombody you want to invite to your party: ")
    print(name, "has now been invited")
    count = count + 1
    again = input("Do you want to invite somebody else? (y/n) ")
print("You have", count, "people coming to your party")
```

049

```python
compnum = 50
guess = int(input("Can you guess the number I am thinking of? "))
count = 1
while guess != compnum:
    if guess < compnum:
        print("Too low")
    else:
        print("Too high")
    count = count+1
    guess = int(input("Have another guess: "))
print("Well done, you took", count, "attempts")
```

050

```python
num = int(input("Enter a number between 10 and 20: "))
while num <10 or num >20:
    if num <10:
        print("Too low")
    else:
        print("Too high")
    num = int(input("Try again: "))
print("Thank you")
```

051

```python
num = 10
while num >0:
    print("There are ", num, "green bottles hanging on the wall.")
    print( num, "green bottles hanging on the wall.")
    print("And if 1 green bottle should accidentally fall,")
    num = num - 1
    answer = int(input("How many green bottles will be hanging on the wall? "))
    if answer == num:
        print("There will be", num, "green bottles hanging on the wall.")
    else:
        while answer!=num:
            answer = int(input("No, try again: "))
print("There are no more green bottles hanging on the wall.")
```

Random

Explanation

Python can generate **random** values. In reality, the values are not completely random as no computer can cope with that; instead it uses an incredibly complex algorithm that makes it virtually impossible to accurately predict its outcome so, in effect, it acts like a random function.

There are two types of random value that we will be looking at:

• Random numbers within a specified range;

• A random choice from a range of items that are input.

 To use these two options, you will need to import the random library. You do this by typing **import random** at the start of your program.

Example Code

`import random`
This must appear at the start of your program otherwise the random function will not work.

`num = random.random()`
Selects a random floating-point number between 0 and 1 and stores it in a variable called "num". If you want to obtain a larger number, you can multiply it as shown below:

```
import random
num = random.random()
num = num * 100
print(num)
```

`num = random.randint(0,9)`
Selects a random whole number between 0 and 9 (inclusive).

`num1 = random.randint(0,1000)`
`num2 = random.randint(0,1000)`
`newrand = num1/num2`
`print(newrand)`
Creates a random floating-point number by creating two random integers within two large ranges (in this case between 0 and 1000) and dividing one by the other.

You are doing great!

`num = random.randrange(0,100,5)`
Picks a random number between the numbers 0 and 100 (inclusive) in steps of five, i.e. it will only pick from 0, 5, 10, 15, 20, etc.

`colour = random.choice(["red","black","green"])`
Picks a random value from the options "red", "black" or "green" and stores it as the variable "colour". Remember: strings need to include speech marks but numeric data does not.

Challenges

052
Display a random integer between 1 and 100 inclusive.

053
Display a random fruit from a list of five fruits.

054
Randomly choose either heads or tails ("h" or "t"). Ask the user to make their choice. If their choice is the same as the randomly selected value, display the message "You win", otherwise display "Bad luck". At the end, tell the user if the computer selected heads or tails.

055

Randomly choose a number between 1 and 5. Ask the user to pick a number. If they guess correctly, display the message "Well done", otherwise tell them if they are too high or too low and ask them to pick a second number. If they guess correctly on their second guess, display "Correct", otherwise display "You lose".

056
Randomly pick a whole number between 1 and 10. Ask the user to enter a number and keep entering numbers until they enter the number that was randomly picked.

057
Update program 056 so that it tells the user if they are too high or too low before they pick again.

058
Make a maths quiz that asks five questions by randomly generating two whole numbers to make the question (e.g. [num1] + [num2]). Ask the user to enter the answer. If they get it right add a point to their score. At the end of the quiz, tell them how many they got correct out of five.

059
Display five colours and ask the user to pick one. If they pick the same as the program has chosen, say "Well done", otherwise display a witty answer which involves the correct colour, e.g. "I bet you are GREEN with envy" or "You are probably feeling BLUE right now". Ask them to guess again; if they have still not got it right, keep giving them the same clue and ask the user to enter a colour until they guess it correctly.

Answers

052

```python
import random
num = random.randint(1,100)
print(num)
```

053

```python
import random
fruit = random.choice( ['apple', 'orange', 'grape', 'banana', 'strawberry'] )
print(fruit)
```

054

```python
import random
coin = random.choice( ["h", "t"] )
guess = input("Enter (h)eads or (t)ails: ")
if guess == coin:
    print("You win")
else:
    print("Bad luck")
if coin == "h":
    print("It was heads")
else:
    print("It was tails")
```

055

```python
import random
num = random.randint(1,5)
guess = int(input("Enter a number: "))
if guess == num:
    print("Well done")
elif guess > num:
    print("Too high")
    guess = int(input("Guess again: "))
    if guess == num:
        print("Correct")
    else:
        print("You lose")
elif guess < num:
    print("Too low")
    guess = int(input("Guess again: "))
    if guess == num:
        print("Correct")
    else:
        print("You lose")
```

056

```python
import random
num = random.randint(1,10)
correct = False
while correct == False:
    guess = int(input("Enter a number: "))
    if guess == num:
        correct = True
```

057

```python
import random
num = random.randint(1,10)
correct = False
while correct == False:
    guess = int(input("Enter a number: "))
    if guess == num:
        correct = True
    elif guess > num:
        print("Too high")
    else:
        print("Too low")
```

058

```python
import random
score = 0
for i in range(1,6):
    num1 = random.randint(1,50)
    num2 = random.randint(1,50)
    correct = num1 + num2
    print(num1, "+", num2,"= ")
    answer = int(input("Your answer: "))
    print()
    if answer == correct:
        score = score + 1
print("You scored",score, "out of 5")
```

059

```python
import random

colour = random.choice(["red","blue","green","white", "pink"])
print("Select from red, blue, green, white or pink")
tryagain = True
while tryagain == True:
    theirchoice = input("Enter a colour: ")
    theirchoice = theirchoice.lower()
    if colour == theirchoice:
        print("Well done")
        tryagain = False
    else:
        if colour == "red":
            print("I bet you are seeing RED right now!")
        elif colour == "blue":
            print("Don't feel BLUE.")
        elif colour == "green":
            print("I bet you are GREEN with envy right now.")
        elif colour == "white":
            print("Are you WHITE as a sheet, as you didn't guess correctly?")
        elif colour == "pink":
            print("Shame you are not feeling in the PINK, as you got it wrong!")
```

Turtle Graphics

Explanation

It is possible to draw using a **turtle** in Python. By typing in commands and using loops, you can create intricate patterns. Here is how it works.

A turtle will travel along a path that you define, leaving a pen mark behind it. As you control the turtle, the pattern that is left is revealed. To draw the pentagon shown below you would type in the following code.

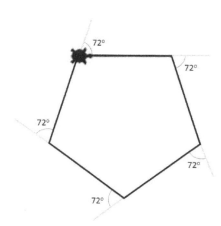

```
import turtle

turtle.shape("turtle")

for i in range(0,5):
    turtle.forward(100)
    turtle.right(72)

turtle.exitonclick()
```

By combining these simple shapes and using **nested** loops (i.e. loops inside other loops) it is possible to create beautiful patterns very easily.

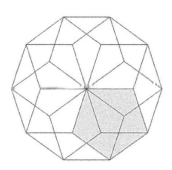

```
import turtle

for i in range(0,10):
    turtle.right(36)
    for i in range(0,5):
        turtle.forward(100)
        turtle.right(72)

turtle.exitonclick()
```

In the above pattern, one pentagon has been repeatedly drawn 10 times, rotating 36 degrees around a central point. **Please note:** we have highlighted one of the pentagons to help you identify it within the pattern, but it would not usually be highlighted.

Example Code

import turtle
This line needs to be included at the beginning of your program to import the turtle library into Python, allowing you to use the turtle functions.

scr = turtle.Screen()
Defines the window as being called "scr". This means we can use the shorthand "scr", rather than having to refer to the window by its full name each time.

scr.bgcolor("yellow")
Sets the screen background colour to yellow. By default, the background colour will be white unless it is changed.

turtle.penup()
Removes the pen from the page so that as the turtle moves it does not leave a trail behind it.

turtle.pendown()
Places the pen on the page so that when the turtle moves it will leave a trail behind it. By default, the pen is down unless specified otherwise.

turtle.pensize(3)
Changes the turtle pen size (the thickness of the line that is drawn) to 3. By default, this is 1 unless it is changed.

turtle.left(120)
Turns the turtle 120° to the left (counter clockwise).

turtle.right(90)
Turns the turtle 90° to the right (clockwise).

turtle.forward(50)
Moves the turtle forward 50 steps.

turtle.shape("turtle")
Changes the shape of the turtle to look like a turtle 🐢. By default, the turtle will look like a small arrow.

turtle.hideturtle()
Hides the turtle so it is not showing on the screen.

turtle.begin_fill()
Entered before the code that draws a shape so it knows to fill in the shape it is drawing.

turtle.showturtle()
Shows the turtle on the screen. By default, the turtle is showing unless specified otherwise.

turtle.end_fill()
Entered after the code that is drawing the shape to tell Python to stop filling in the shape.

turtle.color("black","red")
Defines the colours filling in the shape. This example will make the shape have a black outline and a red fill. This needs to be entered before the shape is drawn.

turtle.exitonclick()
When the user clicks on the turtle window it will automatically close.

Challenges

Don't forget that you can reuse previous programs to save time when you are making new programs. Simply use SAVE AS and give it a new name.

060
Draw a square.

061
Draw a triangle.

062
Draw a circle.

063
Draw three squares in a row with a gap between each. Fill them using three different colours.

065
Write the numbers as shown below, starting at the bottom of the number one.

064
Draw a five-pointed star.

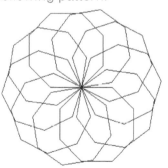

066
Draw an octagon that uses a different colour (randomly selected from a list of six possible colours) for each line.

067
Create the following pattern:

068
Draw a pattern that will change each time the program is run. Use the random function to pick the number of lines, the length of each line and the angle of each turn.

Your programming skills are growing with every challenge you complete.

Answers

060

```
import turtle

for i in range(0,4):
    turtle.forward(100)
    turtle.right(90)

turtle.exitonclick()
```

061

```
import turtle

for i in range (0,3):
    turtle.forward(100)
    turtle.left(120)

turtle.exitonclick()
```

062

```
import turtle

for i in range (0,360):
    turtle.forward(1)
    turtle.right(1)

turtle.exitonclick()
```

063

```python
import turtle

turtle.color("black","red")
turtle.begin_fill()
for i in range (0,4):
    turtle.forward(70)
    turtle.right(90)
turtle.penup()
turtle.end_fill()
turtle.forward(100)

turtle.pendown()
turtle.color("black","yellow")
turtle.begin_fill()
for i in range (0,4):
    turtle.forward(70)
    turtle.right(90)
turtle.penup()
turtle.end_fill()
turtle.forward(100)

turtle.pendown()
turtle.color("black","green")
turtle.begin_fill()
for i in range (0,4):
    turtle.forward(70)
    turtle.right(90)
turtle.end_fill()

turtle.exitonclick()
```

064

```python
import turtle

for i in range (0,5):
    turtle.forward(100)
    turtle.right(144)

turtle.exitonclick()
```

065

```python
import turtle

turtle.left(90)
turtle.forward(100)
turtle.right(90)
turtle.penup()
turtle.forward(50)
turtle.pendown()
turtle.forward(75)
turtle.right(90)
turtle.forward(50)
turtle.right(90)
turtle.forward(75)
turtle.left(90)
turtle.forward(50)
turtle.left(90)
turtle.forward(75)
turtle.penup()
turtle.forward(50)
turtle.pendown()
turtle.forward(75)
turtle.left(90)
turtle.forward(50)
turtle.left(90)
turtle.forward(45)
turtle.left(180)
turtle.forward(45)
turtle.left(90)
turtle.forward(50)
turtle.left(90)
turtle.forward(75)

turtle.hideturtle()

turtle.exitonclick()
```

066

```
import turtle
import random

turtle.pensize(3)

for i in range (0,8):
    turtle.color(random.choice( ["red","blue","yellow","green","pink","orange"]))
    turtle.forward(50)
    turtle.right(45)

turtle.exitonclick()
```

067

```
import turtle
import random

for x in range(0,10):
    for i in range (0,8):
        turtle.forward(50)
        turtle.right(45)
    turtle.right(36)

turtle.hideturtle()

turtle.exitonclick()
```

068

```
import turtle
import random

lines = random.randint(5,20)

for x in range(0,lines):
    length = random.randint(25,100)
    rotate = random.randint(1,365)
    turtle.forward(length)
    turtle.right(rotate)

turtle.exitonclick()
```

Tuples, Lists and Dictionaries

Explanation

So far, we have used variables that can store a single item of data in them. When you used the **random.choice(["red", "blue", "green"])** line of code you are picking a random item from a list of possible options. This demonstrates that one item can hold several pieces of separate data, in this case a collection of colours.

There are several ways that collections of data can be stored as a single item. Three of the simpler ones are:

- tuples

- lists

- dictionaries

Tuples

Once a **tuple** is defined you cannot change what is stored in it. This means that when you write the program you must state what the data is that is being stored in the tuple and the data cannot be altered while the program is running. Tuples are usually used for menu items that would not need to be changed.

Lists

The contents of a **list** can be changed while the program is running and lists are one of the most common ways to store a collection of data under one variable name in Python. The data in a list does not all have to be of the same data type. For example, the same list can store both strings and integers; however, this can cause problems later and is therefore not recommended.

☞ **Please note:** In other programming languages the term **array** is often used to describe a variable that contains a collection of data, and these work in a similar way to lists in Python. There is a data type called an array in Python, but this is only used to store numbers and we will look at Python numeric arrays on page 72.

Dictionaries

The contents of a **dictionary** can also be changed while the program is running. Each value is given an index or key you can define to help identify each piece of data. This index will not change if other rows of data are added or deleted, unlike lists where the position of the items can change and therefore their index number will also change.

Don't get yourself in a tangle, take each program and break it into the parts you already know from previous programs and build in the new skills you are learning.

Example Code

`fruit_tuple = ("apple","banana","strawberry","orange")`
Creates a variable name called "fruit_tuple" which stores four pieces of fruit within it. The round brackets define this group as a tuple and therefore the contents of this collection of data cannot be altered while the program is running.

`print(fruit_tuple.index("strawberry"))`
Displays the index (i.e. the numeric key) of the item "strawberry". In this example it will return the number 2 as Python starts counting the items from 0, not 1.

`print(fruit_tuple[2])`
Displays item 2 from "fruit_tuple", in this case "strawberry".

`names_list = ["John","Tim","Sam"]`
Creates a list of the names and stores them in the variable "names_list". The square brackets define this group of data as a list and therefore the contents can be altered while the program is running.

`del names_list[1]`
Deletes item 1 from "names_list". Remember it starts counting from 0 and not 1. In this case it will delete "Tim" from the list.

`names_list.append(input("Add a name: "))`
Asks the user to enter a name and will add that to the end of "names_list".

`print(sorted(names_list))`
Displays names_list in alphabetical order but does not change the order of the original list, which is still saved in the original order. This does not work if the list is storing data of different types, such as strings and numeric data in the same list.

`names_list.sort()`
Sorts name_list into alphabetical order and saves the list in the new order. This does not work if the list is storing data of different types, such as strings and numeric data in the same list.

`colours = {1:"red",2:"blue",3:"green"}`
Creates a dictionary called "colours", where each item is assigned an index of your choosing. The first item in each block is the index, separated by a colon and then the colour.

`colours[2] = "yellow"`
Makes a change to the data stored in position 2 of the colours dictionary. In this case it will change "blue" to "yellow".

As lists are one of the most common data structures we include more example code just for lists.

```
x = [154,634,892,345,341,43]
```
Here we have created a list that contains numbers. **Please note:** as it contains numeric data, no speech marks are required.

```
print(len(x))
```
Displays the length of the list (i.e. how many items are in the list).

```
print(x[1:4])
```
This will display data in positions 1, 2 and 3. In this case 634, 892 and 345. Remember, Python starts counting from 0 and will stop when it gets to the last position, without showing the final value.

```
for i in x:
 print(i)
```
Uses the items in the list in a for loop, useful if you want to print the items in a list on separate lines.

```
num = int(input("Enter number: "))
if num in x:
 print(num,"is in the list")
else:
 print("Not in the list")
```
Asks the user to enter a number and checks whether the number is in the list and displays an appropriate message.

```
x.insert(2,420)
```
Inserts the number 420 into position 2 and pushes everything else along to make space. This will change the index numbers of the items in the list.

```
x.remove(892)
```
Deletes an item from the list. This is useful if you do not know the index of that item. If there is more than one instance of the data it will only delete the first instance.

```
x.append(993)
```
Adds the number 993 to the end of the list.

Challenges

069

Create a tuple containing the names of five countries and display the whole tuple. Ask the user to enter one of the countries that have been shown to them and then display the index number (i.e. position in the list) of that item in the tuple.

070

Add to program 069 to ask the user to enter a number and display the country in that position.

071

Create a list of two sports. Ask the user what their favourite sport is and add this to the end of the list. Sort the list and display it.

072

Create a list of six school subjects. Ask the user which of these subjects they don't like. Delete the subject they have chosen from the list before you display the list again.

073

Ask the user to enter four of their favourite foods and store them in a dictionary so that they are indexed with numbers starting from 1. Display the dictionary in full, showing the index number and the item. Ask them which they want to get rid of and remove it from the list. Sort the remaining data and display the dictionary.

074

Enter a list of ten colours. Ask the user for a starting number between 0 and 4 and an end number between 5 and 9. Display the list for those colours between the start and end numbers the user input.

075

Create a list of four three-digit numbers. Display the list to the user, showing each item from the list on a separate line. Ask the user to enter a three-digit number. If the number they have typed in matches one in the list, display the position of that number in the list, otherwise display the message "That is not in the list".

076

Ask the user to enter the names of three people they want to invite to a party and store them in a list. After they have entered all three names, ask them if they want to add another. If they do, allow them to add more names until they answer "no". When they answer "no", display how many people they have invited to the party.

077

Change program 076 so that once the user has completed their list of names, display the full list and ask them to type in one of the names on the list. Display the position of that name in the list. Ask the user if they still want that person to come to the party. If they answer "no", delete that entry from the list and display the list again.

You are over halfway there. Keep going, you have already learnt so much.

078

Create a list containing the titles of four TV programmes and display them on separate lines. Ask the user to enter another show and a position they want it inserted into the list. Display the list again, showing all five TV programmes in their new positions.

079

Create an empty list called "nums". Ask the user to enter numbers. After each number is entered, add it to the end of the nums list and display the list. Once they have entered three numbers, ask them if they still want the last number they entered saved. If they say "no", remove the last item from the list. Display the list of numbers.

Answers

069

```
country_tuple = ("France","England","Spain","Germany","Australia")
print(country_tuple)
print()
country = input("Please enter one of the countries from above: ")
print(country, "has index number",country_tuple.index(country))
```

070

```
country_tuple = ("France","England","Spain","Germany","Australia")
print(country_tuple)
print()
country = input("Please enter one of the countries from above: ")
print(country, "has index number",country_tuple.index(country))
print()
num = int(input("Enter a number betwen 0 and 4: "))
print(country_tuple[num])
```

071

```
sports_list = ["tennis","football"]
sports_list.append(input("What is your favourite sport? "))
sports_list.sort()
print(sports_list)
```

072

```
subject_list = ["maths","english","computing","history","science","spanish"]
print(subject_list)
dislike = input("Which of these subjects do you dislike? ")
getrid = subject_list.index(dislike)
del subject_list[getrid]
print(subject_list)
```

073

```
food_dictionary = {}
food1 = input("Enter a food you like: ")
food_dictionary[1] = food1
food2 = input("Enter another food you like: ")
food_dictionary[2] = food2
food3 = input("Enter a third food you like: ")
food_dictionary[3] = food3
food4 = input("Enter one last food you like: ")
food_dictionary[4] = food4
print(food_dictionary)
dislike = int(input("Which of these do you want to get rid of? "))
del food_dictionary[dislike]
print(sorted(food_dictionary.values()))
```

074

```
colours = ["red","blue","green","black","white","pink","grey","purple","yellow","brown"]
start = int(input("Enter a starting number (0-4): "))
end = int(input("Enter an end number (5-9): "))
print(colours[start:end])
```

075

```
nums = [123,345,234,765]
for i in nums:
    print(i)
selection = int(input("Enter a number from the list: "))
if selection in nums:
    print(selection,"is in position",nums.index(selection))
else:
    print("That is not in the list")
```

076

```
name1 = input("Enter a name of somebody you want to invite to your party: ")
name2 = input("Enter another name: ")
name3 = input("Enter a third name: ")
party = [name1,name2,name3]
another = input("Do you want to invite another (y/n): ")
while another == "y":
    newname = party.append(input("Enter another name: "))
    another = input("Do you want to invite another (y/n): ")
print("You have", len(party), "people coming to your party")
```

077

```
name1 = input("Enter a name of somebody you want to invite to your party: ")
name2 = input("Enter another name: ")
name3 = input("Enter a third name: ")
party = [name1,name2,name3]
another = input("Do you want to invite another (y/n): ")
while another == "y":
    newname = party.append(input("Enter another name: "))
    another = input("Do you want to invite another (y/n): ")
print("You have", len(party), "people coming to your party")
print(party)
selection = input("Enter one of the names: ")
print(selection,"is in position",party.index(selection),"on the list")
stillcome = input("Do you still want them to come (y/n): ")
if stillcome == "n":
    party.remove(selection)
print(party)
```

078

```
tv = ["Task Master","Top Gear","The Big Bang Theory","How I Met Your Mother"]
for i in tv:
    print (i)
print()
newtv = input("Enter another TV show: ")
position = int(input("Enter a number between 0 and 3: "))
tv.insert(position,newtv)
for i in tv:
    print (i)
```

079

```
nums = []
count = 0
while count <3:
    num = int(input("Enter a number: "))
    nums.append(num)
    print(nums)
    count = count + 1
lastnum = input("Do you want the last number saved (y/n): ")
if lastnum == "n":
    nums.remove(num)
print(nums)
```

More String Manipulation

Explanation

A **string** is the technical name for a group of characters that you *do not need to perform calculations with*. "Hello" would be an example of a string, as would "7B".

Here we have a variable called **name** which is assigned the value "Simon".

```
name = "Simon"
```

"Simon" can be thought of as a sequence of individual characters and each character in that string can be identified by its index.

Index	0	1	2	3	4
Value	S	i	m	o	n

Note how strings start indexing from 0 and not 1, just as lists do. If the string had a space in it, the space would also be counted as a character, as would any puncluation in the string.

Index	0	1	2	3	4	5	6	7	8	9	10	11
Value	H	e	l	l	o		W	o	r	l	d	!

Now you are familiar with dealing with lists, strings should hold no problems for you as they use the same methods you have used with lists. However, I have included some additional code which may prove useful.

Example Code

Please note: in the examples below, "msg" is a variable name containing a string.

```
if msg.isupper():
 print("Uppercase")
else:
 print("This is not in uppercase")
```
If the message is in uppercase it will display the message "Uppercase", otherwise it will display the message "This is not in uppercase".

```
msg.islower()
```
Can be used in place of the isupper () function to check if the variable contains lower case letters.

```
msg="Hello"
for letter in msg:
 print(letter,end="*")
```
Displays the message, and between each character it will display a "*".
The output in this example will be: **H*e*l*l*o***

Remember, you can always look back on previous programs to remind yourself of the skills learnt earlier.

Challenges

080

Ask the user to enter their first name and then display the length of their first name. Then ask for their surname and display the length of their surname. Join their first name and surname together with a space between and display the result. Finally, display the length of their full name (including the space).

081

Ask the user to type in their favourite school subject. Display it with "-" after each letter, e.g. S-p-a-n-i-s-h-.

082

Show the user a line of text from your favourite poem and ask for a starting and ending point. Display the characters between those two points.

083

Ask the user to type in a word in upper case. If they type it in lower case, ask them to try again. Keep repeating this until they type in a message all in uppercase.

084

Ask the user to type in their postcode. Display the first two letters in uppercase.

085

Ask the user to type in their name and then tell them how many vowels are in their name.

086

Ask the user to enter a new password. Ask them to enter it again. If the two passwords match, display "Thank you". If the letters are correct but in the wrong case, display the message "They must be in the same case", otherwise display the message "Incorrect".

087

Ask the user to type in a word and then display it backwards on separate lines. For instance, if they type in "Hello" it should display as shown below:

```
Enter a word: Hello
o
l
l
e
H
>>>
```

Answers

080

```python
fname = input("Enter your first name: ")
print("That has", len(fname),"characters in it")
sname = input("Enter your surname: ")
print("That has", len(sname),"characters in it")
name = fname + " " + sname
print("Your full name is",name)
print("That has", len(name),"characters in it")
```

081

```python
subject = input("Enter your favourite school subject: ")
for letter in subject:
    print(letter,end = "-")
```

082

```python
poem = "Oh, I wish I'd looked after me teeth,"
print(poem)
start = int(input("Enter a starting number: "))
end = int(input("Enter an end number: "))
print(poem[start:end])
```

083

```python
msg = input("Enter a message in uppercase: ")
tryagain = False
while tryagain == False:
    if msg.isupper():
        print("Thank you")
        tryagain = True
    else:
        print("Try again")
        msg = input("Enter a message in uppercase: ")
```

084

```python
postcode = input("Enter your postcode: ")
start = postcode[0:2]
print(start.upper())
```

085

```python
name = input("Enter your name: ")
count = 0
name = name.lower()
for x in name:
    if x == "a" or x == "e" or x == "i" or x == "o" or x == "u":
        count = count + 1
print("Vowels =", count)
```

086

```python
pswd1 = input("Enter a password: ")
pswd2 = input("Enter it again: ")
if pswd1 == pswd2:
    print("Thank you")
elif pswd1.lower() == pswd2.lower():
    print("They must be the same case")
else:
    print("Incorrect")
```

087

```python
word = input("Enter a word: ")
length = len(word)
num = 1
for x in word:
    position = length - num
    letter = word[position]
    print(letter)
    num = num + 1
```

Numeric Arrays

Explanation

Earlier in the book we looked at lists (see page 58). Lists can store a jumble of different types of data at the same time, including strings and numbers. Python **arrays** are similar to lists, but they are **only used to store numbers**. Numbers can have varying ranges, but in an array all pieces of data in that array **must have the same data type,** as outlined in the table below.

Type code	Common name	Description	Size in bytes
'i'	Integer	Whole number between -32,768 and 32,767	2
'l'	Long	Whole number between -2,147,483,648 and 2,147,483,647	4
'f'	Floating-point	Allows decimal places with numbers ranging from -10^{38} to 10^{38} (i.e. allows up to 38 numeric characters including a single decimal point anywhere in that number and can be negative or positive value)	4
'd'	Double	Allows decimal places with numbers ranging from -10^{308} to 10^{308}	8

When you create your array you need to define the type of data it will contain. You cannot alter or change this while the program is running. Therefore, if you define an array as an 'i' type (this allows whole numbers between the values −32,768 and 32,767) you cannot add a decimal point to a number in that array later as it will cause an error message and crash the program.

Please note: Other programming languages use the term array to allow the storage of any data type, but in Python arrays only store numbers whereas lists allow the storage of any data type. If you want to create a variable that stores multiple strings, in Python you need to create a list rather than an array.

Example Code

```
from array import *
```
This needs to be the first line of your program so that
Python can use the array library.

```
nums = array ('i',[45,324,654,45,264])
print(nums)
```
Creates an array called "nums". It uses the integer data type and has five items in the
array. It will display the following as the output:
```
array('i', [45, 324, 654, 45, 264])
```

```
for x in nums:
 print(x)
```
Displays the array with
each item appearing on
a separate line.

```
newValue = int(input("Enter number: "))
nums.append(newValue)
```
Asks the user to enter a new number which it will add to
the end of the existing array.

```
nums.reverse()
```
Reverses the order of
the array.

```
nums = sorted(nums)
```
Sorts the array into
ascending order.

```
nums.pop()
```
This will remove the last
item from the array.

```
newArray = array('i',[])
more = int(input("How many items: "))
for y in range(0,more):
 newValue=int(input("Enter num: "))
 newArray.append(newValue)
nums.extend(newArray)
```
Creates a blank array called "newArray" which uses the
integer data type. It asks the user how many items they
want to add and then appends these new items to
newArray. After all the items have been added it will join
together the contents of newArray and the nums array.

```
getRid = int(input("Enter item index: "))
nums.remove(getRid)
```
Asks the user to enter the item they want to get rid of and then removes the first item
that matches that value from the array.

```
print(nums.count(45))
```
This will display how many times the value "45" appears in the array.

Challenges

088

Ask the user for a list of five integers. Store them in an array. Sort the list and display it in reverse order.

089

Create an array which will store a list of integers. Generate five random numbers and store them in the array. Display the array (showing each item on a separate line).

090

Ask the user to enter numbers. If they enter a number between 10 and 20, save it in the array, otherwise display the message "Outside the range". Once five numbers have been successfully added, display the message "Thank you" and display the array with each item shown on a separate line.

091

Create an array which contains five numbers (two of which should be repeated). Display the whole array to the user. Ask the user to enter one of the numbers from the array and then display a message saying how many times that number appears in the list.

092

Create two arrays (one containing three numbers that the user enters and one containing a set of five random numbers). Join these two arrays together into one large array. Sort this large array and display it so that each number appears on a separate line.

Keep going!

093

Ask the user to enter five numbers. Sort them into order and present them to the user. Ask them to select one of the numbers. Remove it from the original array and save it in a new array.

094

Display an array of five numbers. Ask the user to select one of the numbers. Once they have selected a number, display the position of that item in the array. If they enter something that is not in the array, ask them to try again until they select a relevant item.

095

Create an array of five numbers between 10 and 100 which each have two decimal places. Ask the user to enter a whole number between 2 and 5. If they enter something outside of that range, display a suitable error message and ask them to try again until they enter a valid amount. Divide each of the numbers in the array by the number the user entered and display the answers shown to two decimal places.

Answers

088

```python
from array import *

nums = array('i',[])

for i in range (0,5):
    num = int(input("Enter a number: "))
    nums.append(num)

nums = sorted(nums)
nums.reverse()

print(nums)
```

089

```python
from array import *
import random

nums = array('i',[])

for i in range (0,5):
    num = random.randint(1,100)
    nums.append(num)

for i in nums:
    print(i)
```

090

```python
from array import *

nums = array('i',[])

while len(nums) < 5:
    num = int(input("Enter a number between 10 and 20: "))
    if num >= 10 and num <= 20:
        nums.append(num)
    else:
        print("Outside the range")

for i in nums:
    print(i)
```

091

```
from array import *

nums = array('i',[5,7,9,2,9])

for i in nums:
    print(i)

num = int(input("Enter a number: "))

if nums.count(num) == 1:
    print(num, "is in the list once")
else:
    print(num, "is in the list", nums.count(num),"times")
```

092

```
from array import *
import random

num1 = array('i',[])
num2 = array('i',[])

for i in range(0,3):
    num = int(input("Enter a number: "))
    num1.append(num)

for i in range(0,5):
    num = random.randint(1,100)
    num2.append(num)

num1.extend(num2)

num1 = sorted(num1)

for i in num1:
    print(i)
```

093

```
from array import *

nums = array('i',[])

for i in range(0,5):
    num = int(input("Enter a number: "))
    nums.append(num)

nums = sorted(nums)

for i in nums:
    print(i)

num = int(input("Select a number from the array: "))
if num in nums:
    nums.remove(num)
    num2 = array('i',[])
    num2.append(num)
    print(nums)
    print(num2)
else:
    print("That is not a value in the array")
```

094

```
from array import *

nums = array('i',[4,6,8,2,5])

for i in nums:
    print(i)

num = int(input("Select one of the numbers: "))

tryagain = True
while tryagain == True:
    if num in nums:
        print("This is in position",nums.index(num))
        tryagain = False
    else:
        print("Not in array")
        num = int(input("Select one of the numbers: "))
```

095

```
from array import *
import math

nums = array('f',[34.75,27.23,99.58,45.26,28.65])
tryagain = True
while tryagain == True:
    num = int(input("Enter a number between 2 and 5: "))
    if num<2 or num >5:
        print("Incorrect value, try again.")
    else:
        tryagain = False
for i in range(0,5):
    ans = nums[i]/num
    print(round(ans,2))
```

2D Lists and Dictionaries

Explanation

Technically it is possible to create a two-dimensional array in Python, but as Python arrays are limited to storing numbers and most Python programmers feel more comfortable with working with lists, 2D arrays are rarely used and **2D lists** are far more common.

 Imagine, for one terrifying moment, you are a teacher. Scary I know! Also imagine you have four students and you teach those same students across three different subjects. You may, if you are a conscientious teacher, need to keep records of those students' grades for each of their subjects. It is possible to create a simple chart on paper to do this as follows:

	Maths	English	French
Susan	45	37	54
Peter	62	58	59
Mark	49	47	60
Andy	78	83	62

Two-dimensional lists work in a similar way.

	0	1	2
0	45	37	54
1	62	58	59
2	49	47	60
3	78	83	62

In Python, this two-dimensional list would be coded as follows:

```
grades = [[45,37,54],[62,58,59],[49,47,60],[78,83,62]]
```

Alternatively, if you do not want to use the standard Python column index numbers you can use a dictionary as follows:

```
grades = [{"Ma":45,"En":37,"Fr":54},{"Ma":62,"En":58,"Fr":59},{"Ma":49,"En":47,"Fr":60}]
print(grades[0]["En"])
```

This program will produce the output 37 (the English grade for the pupil with the index number 0) and can make the data easier to understand.

You can even go further and add a row index as follows:

```
grades = {"Susan":{"Ma":45,"En":37,"Fr":54},"Peter":{"Ma":62,"En":58,"Fr":59}}
print(grades["Peter"]["En"])
```

This will give the output 58, the grade for Peter's English exam.

Example Code

	0	1	2
0	2	5	8
1	3	7	4
2	1	6	9

```
simple_array = [[2,5,8],[3,7,4],[1,6,9]]
```
Creates a 2D list (as shown on the right) which uses standard Python indexing for the rows and columns.

```
print(simple_array)
```
Displays all the data in the 2D list.

```
print(simple_array[1])
```
Displays data from row 1, in this case [3, 7, 4].

```
simple_array[2][1]= 5
```
Changes the data in row 2, column 1 to the value 5.

```
print(simple_array[1][2])
```
Displays data from row 1, column 2, in this case 4.

```
simple_array[1].append(3)
```
Adds the value 3 onto the end of the data in row 1 so in this case it becomes [3, 7, 4, 3].

	x	y	z
A	54	82	91
B	75	29	80

```
data_set = {"A":{"x":54,"y":82,"z":91},"B":{"x":75,"y":29,"z":80}}
```
Creates a 2D dictionary using user-defined labels for the rows and columns (as shown above).

```
print(data_set["A"])
```
Displays data from data set "A".

```
print(data_set["B"]["y"])
```
Displays data from row "B", column "y".

```
for i in data_set:
 print(data_set [i]["y"])
```
Displays the "y" column from each row.

```
data_set["B"]["y"] = 53
```
Changes the data in "B", "y", to 53.

```
grades[name]={"Maths":mscore,"English":escore}
```
Adds another row of data to a 2D dictionary. In this case, name would be the row index and Maths and English would be the column indexes.

```
for name in grades:
 print((name),grades[name]["English"])
```
Displays only the name and the English grade for each student.

```
del list[getRid]
```
Removes a selected item.

Challenges

096

Create the following using a simple 2D list using the standard Python indexing:

	0	1	2
0	2	5	8
1	3	7	4
2	1	6	9
3	4	2	0

097

Using the 2D list from program 096, ask the user to select a row and a column and display that value.

098

Using the 2D list from program 096, ask the user which row they would like displayed and display just that row. Ask them to enter a new value and add it to the end of the row and display the row again.

099

Change your previous program to ask the user which row they want displayed. Display that row. Ask which column in that row they want displayed and display the value that is held there. Ask the user if they want to change the value. If they do, ask for a new value and change the data. Finally, display the whole row again.

100

Create the following using a 2D dictionary showing the sales each person has made in the different geographical regions:

	N	S	E	W
John	3056	8463	8441	2694
Tom	4832	6786	4737	3612
Anne	5239	4802	5820	1859
Fiona	3904	3645	8821	2451

101

Using program 100, ask the user for a name and a region. Display the relevant data. Ask the user for the name and region of data they want to change and allow them to make the alteration to the sales figure. Display the sales for all regions for the name they choose.

102

Ask the user to enter the name, age and shoe size for four people. Ask for the name of one of the people in the list and display their age and shoe size.

103

Adapt program 102 to display the names and ages of all the people in the list but do not show their shoe size.

104

After gathering the four names, ages and shoe sizes, ask the user to enter the name of the person they want to remove from the list. Delete this row from the data and display the other rows on separate lines.

Answers

096
```
list = [[2,5,8],[3,7,4],[1,6,9],[4,2,0]]
```

097
```
list = [[2,5,8],[3,7,4],[1,6,9],[4,2,0]]
row = int(input("Select a row: "))
col = int(input("Select a column: "))
print(list[row][col])
```

098
```
list = [[2,5,8],[3,7,4],[1,6,9],[4,2,0]]
row = int(input("Select a row: "))
print(list[row])
newvalue = int(input("Enter a new number: "))
list[row].append(newvalue)
print(list[row])
```

099
```
list = [[2,5,8],[3,7,4],[1,6,9],[4,2,0]]
row = int(input("Select a row: "))
print(list[row])
col = int(input("Select a column: "))
print(list[row][col])
change = input("Do you want to change the value? (y/n) ")
if change == "y":
    newvalue = int(input("Enter new value: "))
    list[row][col] = newvalue
print(list[row])
```

100
Please note the data has been split onto separate rows to make it easier to read the code. This is possible, as long as the breaks are where the rows will natural break and are contained within the curly brackets.

```
sales = {"John":{"N":3056, "S":8463, "E":8441, "W":2694},
"Tom":{"N":4832, "S":6786, "E":4737, "W":3612},
"Anne":{"N":5239, "S":4802, "E":5820, "W":1859},
"Fiona":{"N":3904, "S":3645, "E":8821, "W":2451}}
```

101

```
sales = {"John":{"N":3056, "S":8463, "E":8441, "W":2694},
"Tom":{"N":4832, "S":6786, "E":4737, "W":3612},
"Anne":{"N":5239, "S":4802, "E":5820, "W":1859},
"Fiona":{"N":3904, "S":3645, "E":8821, "W":2451}}
person = input("Enter sales person's name: ")
region = input("Select region: ")
print(sales[person][region])
newdata = int(input("Enter new data: "))
sales[person][region] = newdata
print(sales[person])
```

102

```
list = {}
for i in range (0,4):
    name = input("Enter name: ")
    age = int(input("Enter age: "))
    shoe = int(input("Enter shoe size: "))
    list[name] = {"Age":age,"Shoe size":shoe}

ask = input("Enter a name: ")
print(list[ask])
```

103

```
list = {}
for i in range (0,4):
    name = input("Enter name: ")
    age = int(input("Enter age: "))
    shoe = int(input("Enter shoe size: "))
    list[name] = {"Age":age,"Shoe size":shoe}

for name in list:
    print((name),list[name]["Age"])
```

104

```
list = {}
for i in range (0,4):
    name = input("Enter name: ")
    age = int(input("Enter age: "))
    shoe = int(input("Enter shoe size: "))
    list[name] = {"Age":age,"Shoe size":shoe}

getrid = input("Who do you want to remove from the list? ")
del list[getrid]

for name in list:
    print((name),list[name]["Age"],list[name]["Shoe size"])
```

Reading and Writing to a Text File

Explanation

It is all very well being able to define a list, make changes and add new data, but if the next time the program is run it returns to the original data and your changes are lost then it is not a lot of use. Therefore, it is sometimes necessary to save data outside of the program and this way the data can be stored, along with any changes that are made.

 The easiest place to start learning about writing and reading from an external file is with a **text** file.

When opening an external file you must specify how that file will be used within the program. The options are below.

Code	Description
w	**Write mode:** used to create a new file. Any existing files with the same name will be erased and a new one created in its place.
r	**Read mode:** used when an existing file is only being read and not being written to.
a	**Append mode:** used to add new data to the end of the file.

Text files are only used to write, read and append data. By the very nature of how they work it is not easy to remove or alter individual elements of data once it is written to the file, unless you want to overwrite the entire file or create a new file to store the new data. If you want to be able to alter the individual elements once the file has been created it is better to use a .csv file (see page 91) or an SQL database (see page 134).

Example Code

```
file = open("Countries.txt","w")
file.write("Italy\n")
file.write("Germany\n")
file.write("Spain\n")
file.close()
```
Creates a file called "Countries.txt". If one already exists then it will be overwritten with a new blank file. It will add three lines of data to the file (the \n forces a new line after each entry). It will then close the file, allowing the changes to the text file to be saved.

```
file = open("Countries.txt","r")
print(file.read())
```
This will open the Countries.txt file in "read" mode and display the entire file.

```
file = open("Countries.txt","a")
file.write("France\n")
file.close()
```
This will open the Countries.txt file in "append" mode, add another line and then close the file.

If the **file.close()** line is not included, the changes will not be saved to the text file.

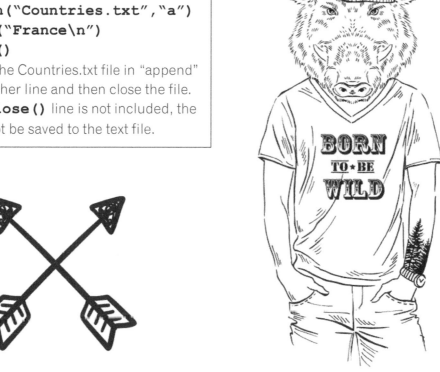

Challenges

105

Write a new file called "Numbers.txt". Add five numbers to the document which are stored on the same line and only separated by a comma. Once you have run the program, look in the location where your program is stored and you should see that the file has been created. The easiest way to view the contents of the new text file on a Windows system is to read it using Notepad.

106

Create a new file called "Names.txt". Add five names to the document, which are stored on separate lines. Once you have run the program, look in the location where your program is stored and check that the file has been created properly.

107

Open the Names.txt file and display the data in Python.

108

Open the Names.txt file. Ask the user to input a new name. Add this to the end of the file and display the entire file.

109

Display the following menu to the user:

```
1) Create a new file
2) Display the file
3) Add a new item to the file
Make a selection 1, 2 or 3:
```

Ask the user to enter 1, 2 or 3. If they select anything other than 1, 2 or 3 it should display a suitable error message.

If they select 1, ask the user to enter a school subject and save it to a new file called "Subject.txt". It should overwrite any existing file with a new file.

If they select 2, display the contents of the "Subject.txt" file.

If they select 3, ask the user to enter a new subject and save it to the file and then display the entire contents of the file.

Run the program several times to test the options.

110

Using the Names.txt file you created earlier, display the list of names in Python. Ask the user to type in one of the names and then save all the names except the one they entered into a new file called Names2.txt.

Fantastic work, saving data to external files is an important programming skill.

Answers

105

```
file = open("Numbers.txt","w")
file.write("4, ")
file.write("6, ")
file.write("10, ")
file.write("8, ")
file.write("5, ")
file.close()
```

106

```
file = open("Names.txt","w")
file.write("Bob\n")
file.write("Tom\n")
file.write("Gemma\n")
file.write("Sarah\n")
file.write("Timothy\n")
file.close()
```

107

```
file = open("Names.txt","r")
print(file.read())
file.close()
```

108

```
file = open("Names.txt", "a")
newname = input("Enter a new name: ")
file.write(newname + "\n")
file.close

file = open("Names.txt", "r")
print (file.read())
file.close
```

109

```python
print ("1) Create a new file")
print ("2) Display the file")
print ("3) Add a new item to the file")
selection = int(input("Make a selection 1, 2 or 3: "))
if selection == 1:
    subject = input("Enter a school subject: ")
    file = open("Subject.txt","w")
    file.write(subject + "\n")
    file.close()
elif selection == 2:
    file = open("Subject.txt","r")
    print(file.read())
elif selection == 3:
    file = open("Subject.txt","a")
    subject = input("Enter a school subject: ")
    file.write(subject + "\n")
    file.close()
    file = open("Subject.txt","r")
    print(file.read())
else:
    print("Invalid option")
```

110

```python
file = open("Names.txt","r")
print(file.read())
file.close()

file = open("Names.txt","r")
selectedname = input("Enter a name from the list: ")
selectedname = selectedname + "\n"
for row in file:
    if row != selectedname:
        file = open("Names2.txt","a")
        newrecord = row
        file.write(newrecord)
        file.close()
file.close()
```

Reading and Writing to a .csv File

Explanation

CSV stands for **Comma Separated Values** and is a format usually associated with importing and exporting from spreadsheets and databases. It allows greater control over the data than a simple text file, as each row is split up into identifiable columns. Below is an example of data you may want to store.

Name	Age	Star sign
Brian	73	Taurus
Sandra	48	Virgo
Zoe	25	Scorpio
Keith	43	Leo

A .csv file would store the above data as follows:

```
Brian, 73, Taurus
Sandra, 48, Virgo
Zoe, 25, Scorpio
Keith, 43, Leo
```

However, it may be easier to think of it as being separated into columns and rows that use an index number to identify them.

	0	1	2
0	Brian	73	Taurus
1	Sandra	48	Virgo
2	Zoe	25	Scorpio
3	Keith	43	Leo

When opening a .csv file to use, you must specify how that file will be used. The options are:

Code	Description
w	Creates a new file and writes to that file. If the file already exists, a new file will be created, overwriting the existing file.
x	Creates a new file and writes to that file. If the file already exists, the program will crash rather than overwrite it.
r	Opens for reading only and will not allow you to make changes.
a	Opens for writing, appending to the end of the file.

Example Code

```
import csv
```
This must be at the top of your program to allow Python to use the .csv library of commands.

```
file = open ("Stars.csv","w")
newRecord = "Brian,73,Taurus\n"
file.write(str(newRecord))
file.close()
```
This will create a new file called "Stars.csv", overwriting any previous files of the same name. It will add a new record and then close and save the changes to the file.

```
file = open ("Stars.csv","a")
name = input("Enter name: ")
age = input("Enter age: ")
star = input("Enter star sign: ")
newRecord = name + "," + age + "," + star + "\n"
file.write(str(newRecord))
file.close()
```
This will open the Stars.csv file, ask the user to enter the name, age and star sign, and will append this to the end of the file.

```
file = open("Stars.csv","r")
for row in file:
 print(row)
```
This will open the Stars.csv file in read mode and display the records one row at a time.

```
file = open("Stars.csv","r")
reader = csv.reader(file)
rows = list(reader)
print(rows[1])
```
This will open the Stars.csv file and display only row 1. Remember, Python starts counting from 0.

```
file = open ("Stars.csv","r")
search = input("Enter the data you are searching for: ")
reader = csv.reader(file)
for row in file:
 if search in str(row):
  print(row)
```
Asks the user to enter the data they are searching for. It will display all rows that contain that data anywhere in that row.

```
import csv
file = list(csv.reader(open("Stars.csv")))
tmp = []
for row in file:
  tmp.append(row)
```
A .csv file cannot be altered, only added to. If you need to alter the file you need to write it to a temporary list. This block of code will read the original .csv file and write it to a list called "tmp". This can then be used and altered as a list (see page 58).

```
file = open("NewStars.csv","w")
x = 0
for row in tmp:
  newRec = tmp[x][0] + "," + tmp[x][1] + "," + tmp[x][2] + "\n"
  file.write(newRec)
  x = x + 1
file.close()
```
Writes from a list into a new .csv file called "NewStars.csv".

Challenges

111

Create a .csv file that will store the following data. Call it "Books.csv".

	Book	Author	Year Released
0	To Kill A Mockingbird	Harper Lee	1960
1	A Brief History of Time	Stephen Hawking	1988
2	The Great Gatsby	F. Scott Fitzgerald	1922
3	The Man Who Mistook His Wife for a Hat	Oliver Sacks	1985
4	Pride and Prejudice	Jane Austen	1813

112

Using the Books.csv file from program 111, ask the user to enter another record and add it to the end of the file. Display each row of the .csv file on a separate line.

113

Using the Books.csv file, ask the user how many records they want to add to the list and then allow them to add that many. After all the data has been added, ask for an author and display all the books in the list by that author. If there are no books by that author in the list, display a suitable message.

114

Using the Books.csv file, ask the user to enter a starting year and an end year. Display all books released between those two years.

115

Using the Books.csv file, display the data in the file along with the row number of each.

116

Import the data from the Books.csv file into a list. Display the list to the user. Ask them to select which row from the list they want to delete and remove it from the list. Ask the user which data they want to change and allow them to change it. Write the data back to the original .csv file, overwriting the existing data with the amended data.

117

Create a simple maths quiz that will ask the user for their name and then generate two random questions. Store their name, the questions they were asked, their answers and their final score in a .csv file. Whenever the program is run it should add to the .csv file and not overwrite anything.

Answers

111

```
import csv

file = open("Books.csv","w")
newrecord = "To Kill A Mockingbird, Harper Lee, 1960\n"
file.write(str(newrecord))
newrecord = "A Brief History of Time, Stephen Hawking, 1988\n"
file.write(str(newrecord))
newrecord = "The Great Gatsby, F. Scott Fitzgerald, 1922\n"
file.write(str(newrecord))
newrecord = "The Man Who Mistook His Wife for a Hat, Oliver Sacks, 1985\n"
file.write(str(newrecord))
newrecord = "Pride and Prejudice, Jane Austen, 1813\n"
file.write(str(newrecord))
file.close()
```

112

```
import csv

file = open("Books.csv","a")
title = input("Enter a title: ")
author = input("Enter author: ")
year = input("Enter the year it was released: ")
newrecord = title + "," + author + ", " + year + "\n"
file.write(str(newrecord))
file.close()

file = open("Books.csv","r")
for row in file:
    print(row)
file.close()
```

113

```
import csv

num = int(input("How many books do you want to add to the list? "))
file = open("Books.csv","a")
for x in range(0,num):
    title = input("Enter a title: ")
    author = input("Enter author: ")
    year = input("Enter the year it was released: ")
    newrecord = title + "," + author + ", " + year + "\n"
    file.write(str(newrecord))
file.close()

searchauthor = input("Enter an authors name to search for: ")

file = open("Books.csv","r")
count = 0
for row in file:
    if searchauthor in str(row):
        print(row)
        count = count + 1
if count == 0:
    print ("There are no books by that author in this list.")
file.close()
```

114

```
import csv

start = int(input("Enter a starting year: "))
end = int(input("Enter an end year: "))

file = list(csv.reader(open("Books.csv")))
tmp = []
for row in file:
    tmp.append(row)

x = 0
for row in tmp:
    if int(tmp[x][2]) >= start and int(tmp[x][2]) <=end:
        print(tmp[x])
    x = x+1
```

115

```
import csv

file = open("Books.csv","r")
x = 0
for row in file:
    display = "Row: " + str(x) + " - " + row
    print(display)
    x = x + 1
```

116

```python
import csv

file = list(csv.reader(open("Books.csv")))
Booklist = []
for row in file:
    Booklist.append(row)

x = 0
for row in Booklist:
    display = x,Booklist[x]
    print(display)
    x = x + 1
getrid = int(input("Enter a row number to delete: "))
del Booklist[getrid]

x = 0
for row in Booklist:
    display = x,Booklist[x]
    print(display)
    x = x + 1
alter = int(input("Enter a row number to alter: "))
x = 0
for row in Booklist[alter]:
    display = x,Booklist[alter][x]
    print(display)
    x = x + 1
part = int(input("Which part do you want to change? "))
newdata = input("Enter new data: ")
Booklist[alter][part] = newdata
print(Booklist[alter])

file = open("Books.csv","w")
x = 0
for row in Booklist:
    newrecord = Booklist[x][0] + ", " + Booklist[x][1] + ", " + Booklist[x][2] + "\n"
    file.write(newrecord)
    x = x+1
file.close()
```

117

```python
import csv
import random

score = 0
name = input("What is your name: ")
q1_num1 = random.randint(10,50)
q1_num2 = random.randint(10,50)
question1 = str(q1_num1) + " + " + str(q1_num2) + " = "
ans1 = int(input(question1))
realans1 = q1_num1+q1_num2
if ans1 == realans1:
    score = score + 1
q2_num1 = random.randint(10,50)
q2_num2 = random.randint(10,50)
question2 = str(q2_num1) + " + " + str(q2_num2) + " = "
ans2 = int(input(question2))
realans2 = q2_num1+q2_num2
if ans2 == realans2:
    score = score + 1

file = open("QuizScore.csv","a")
newrecord = name+","+question1+","+str(ans1)+","+question2+","+str(ans2)+","+str(score)+"\n"
file.write(str(newrecord))

file.close()
```

Subprograms

Explanation

Subprograms are blocks of code which perform specific tasks and can be called upon at any time in the program to run that code.

Advantages

- You can write a block of code and it can be used and re-used at different times during the program.

- It makes the program simpler to understand as the code is grouped together into chunks.

Defining a subprogram and passing variables between subprograms

Below is a simple program that we would normally create without subprograms but have written it with subprograms so you can see how they work:

```python
def get_name():
    user_name = input("Enter your name: ")
    return user_name

def print_Msg(user_name):
    print("Hello", user_name)

def main():
    user_name = get_name()
    print_Msg(user_name)

main()
```

This program uses three subprograms **get_name()**, **print_Msg()** and **main()**.

The **get_name()** subprogram will ask the user to input their name and then it will return the value of the variable "user_name" so that it can be used in another subprogram. This is very important. If you do not return the values, then the values of any variables that were created or altered in that subprogram cannot be used elsewhere in your program.

The **print_Msg()** subprogram will display the message "Hello" and then the user name. The variable "user_name" appears in the brackets as the current value of the variable is being imported into the subprogram so it can be used.

The **main()** subprogram will get the user_name from the **get_name()** subprogram (using the variable user_name) as this was returned from the **get_name()** subprogram. It will then use that user_name variable in the **print_Msg()** subprogram.

The last line "**main()**" is the actual program itself. All this will do is start the **main()** subprogram running.

Obviously, there is no need to create such a convoluted way of performing what is in fact a very simple program, but this is only used as an example of how subprograms are laid out and variables can be used and passed between the subprograms.

Please note: Python does not like surprises, so if you are going to use a subprogram in a program, Python must have read the "**def subprogram_name()**" line before so it knows where to go to find it. If you try to refer to a subprogram before Python has read about it, it panics and will crash. When calling a subprogram, the subprogram must be written **above** the section of code you use to call it. Python will read from the top down and **run** the first line it comes across that has not been indented and does not start with the word def. In the program above this would be **main()**.

Remember: never surprise Python as it will not like it - good advice for life generally.

Example Code

The following examples are all part of the same program and would be displayed in the order shown here.

```
def get_data():
 user_name = input("Enter your name: ")
 user_age = int(input("Enter your age: "))
 data_tuple = (user_name, user_age)
 return data_tuple
```

Defines a subprogram called "get_data()" which will ask the user for their name and age. As we want to send more than one piece of data back to the main program for other parts of the program to use, we have combined them together. The return line can only return a single value, which is why we combined the user_name and user_age variables into a tuple (see page 58) called data_tuple.

```
def message(user_name,user_age):
 if user_age <= 10:
  print("Hi", user_name)
 else:
  print("Hello", user_name)
```

Defines a subprogram called message() which uses two variables that have previously been defined (user_name and user_age).

```
def main():
 user_name,user_age = get_data()
 message(user_name,user_age)
```

Defines a subprogram called main() which obtains the two variables from the get_data() subprogram. These must be labelled in the same order as they were defined in the tuple. It then calls the message() subprogram to run with the two variables.

```
main()
```

Runs the main() subprogram.

Challenges

118

Define a subprogram that will ask the user to enter a number and save it as the variable "num". Define another subprogram that will use "num" and count from 1 to that number.

119

Define a subprogram that will ask the user to pick a low and a high number, and then generate a random number between those two values and store it in a variable called "comp_num".

Define another subprogram that will give the instruction "I am thinking of a number…" and then ask the user to guess the number they are thinking of.

Define a third subprogram that will check to see if the comp_num is the same as the user's guess. If it is, it should display the message "Correct, you win", otherwise it should keep looping, telling the user if they are too low or too high and asking them to guess again until they guess correctly.

120

Display the following menu to the user:

```
1) Addition
2) Subtraction
Enter 1 or 2:
```

If they enter a 1, it should run a subprogram that will generate two random numbers between 5 and 20, and ask the user to add them together. Work out the correct answer and return both the user's answer and the correct answer.

If they entered 2 as their selection on the menu, it should run a subprogram that will generate one number between 25 and 50 and another number between 1 and 25 and ask them to work out num1 minus num2. This way they will not have to worry about negative answers. Return both the user's answer and the correct answer.

Create another subprogram that will check if the user's answer matches the actual answer. If it does, display "Correct", otherwise display a message that will say "Incorrect, the answer is" and display the real answer.

If they do not select a relevant option on the first menu you should display a suitable message.

121

Create a program that will allow the user to easily manage a list of names. You should display a menu that will allow them to add a name to the list, change a name in the list, delete a name from the list or view all the names in the list. There should also be a menu option to allow the user to end the program. If they select an option that is not relevant, then it should display a suitable message. After they have made a selection to either add a name, change a name, delete a name or view all the names, they should see the menu again without having to restart the program. The program should be made as easy to use as possible.

122

Create the following menu:
```
1) Add to file
2) View all records
3) Quit program

Enter the number of your selection:
```

If the user selects 1, allow them to add to a file called Salaries.csv which will store their name and salary. If they select 2 it should display all records in the Salaries.csv file. If they select 3 it should stop the program. If they select an incorrect option they should see an error message. They should keep returning to the menu until they select option 3.

Including menus helps make the program easier to

123

In Python, it is not technically possible to directly delete a record from a .csv file. Instead you need to save the file to a temporary list in Python, make the changes to the list and then overwrite the original file with the temporary list.

Change the previous program to allow you to do this. Your menu should now look like this:

```
1) Add to file
2) View all records
3) Delete a record
4) Quit program

Enter the number of your selection:
```

Answers

118

```python
def ask_value():
    num = int(input("Enter a number: "))
    return num

def count(num):
    n = 1
    while n <= num:
        print(n)
        n = n + 1

def main():
    num = ask_value()
    count(num)

main()
```

119

```python
import random

def pick_num():
    low = int(input("Enter the bottom of the range: "))
    high = int(input("Enter the top of the range: "))
    comp_num = random.randint(low,high)
    return comp_num

def first_guess():
    print("I am thinking of a number...")
    guess = int(input("What am I thinking of: "))
    return guess

def check_answer(comp_num,guess):
    try_again = True
    while try_again == True:
        if comp_num == guess:
            print("Correct, you win.")
            try_again = False
        elif comp_num > guess:
            guess = int(input("Too low, try again: "))
        else:
            guess = int(input("Too high, try again: "))

def main():
    comp_num = pick_num()
    guess = first_guess()
    check_answer(comp_num,guess)

main()
```

120

```python
import random

def addition():
    num1 = random.randint(5,20)
    num2 = random.randint(5,20)
    print(num1, "+", num2, "= ")
    user_answer = int(input("Your answer: "))
    actual_answer = num1 + num2
    answers = (user_answer, actual_answer)
    return answers

def subtraction():
    num3 = random.randint(25,50)
    num4 = random.randint(1,25)
    print(num3, "-",num4,"= ")
    user_answer = int(input("Your answer: "))
    actual_answer = num3 - num4
    answers = (user_answer, actual_answer)
    return answers

def check_answer(user_answer, actual_answer):
    if user_answer == actual_answer:
        print("Correct")
    else:
        print("Incorrect, the answer is", actual_answer)

def main():
    print("1) Addition")
    print("2) Subtraction")
    selection = int(input("Enter 1 or 2: "))
    if selection == 1:
        user_answer, actual_answer = addition()
        check_answer(user_answer,actual_answer)
    elif selection == 2:
        user_answer, actual_answer = subtraction()
        check_answer(user_answer,actual_answer)
    else:
        print("Incorrect selection")

main()
```

121

```python
def add_name():
    name = input("Enter a new name: ")
    names.append(name)
    return names

def change_name():
    num = 0
    for x in names:
        print(num,x)
        num = num + 1
    select_num = int(input("Enter the number of the name you want to change: "))
    name = input("Enter new name: ")
    names[select_num] = name
    return names

def delete_name():
    num = 0
    for x in names:
        print(num,x)
        num = num + 1
    select_num = int(input("Enter the number of the name you want to delete: "))
    del names[select_num]
    return names

def view_names():
    for x in names:
        print(x)
    print()

def main():
    again = "y"
    while again == "y":
        print("1) Add a name")
        print("2) Change a name")
        print("3) Delete a name")
        print("4) View names")
        print("5) Quit")
        selection = int(input("What do you want to do? "))
        if selection == 1:
            names = add_name()
        elif selection == 2:
            names = change_name()
        elif selection == 3:
            names = delete_name()
        elif selection == 4:
            names = view_names()
        elif selection == 5:
            again = "n"
        else:
            print("Incorrect option: ")
        data = (names, again)


names = []
main()
```

122

```python
import csv

def addtofile():
    file = open("Salaries.csv","a")
    name = input("Enter name: ")
    salary = int(input("Enter salary: "))
    newrecord = name + ", " + str(salary) + "\n"
    file.write(str(newrecord))
    file.close()

def viewrecords():
    file = open("Salaries.csv","r")
    for row in file:
        print(row)
    file.close()

tryagain = True
while tryagain == True:
    print("1) Add to file")
    print("2) View all records")
    print("3) Quit program")
    print()
    selection = input("Enter the number of your selection: ")
    if selection == "1":
        addtofile()
    elif selection == "2":
        viewrecords()
    elif selection == "3":
        tryagain = False
    else:
        print("Incorrect option")
```

123

```python
import csv

def addtofile():
    file = open("Salaries.csv","a")
    name = input("Enter name: ")
    salary = int(input("Enter salary: "))
    newrecord = name + ", " + str(salary) + "\n"
    file.write(str(newrecord))
    file.close()

def viewrecords():
    file = open("Salaries.csv","r")
    for row in file:
        print(row)
    file.close()

def deleterecord():
    file = open("Salaries.csv","r")
    x = 0
    tmplist = []
    for row in file:
        tmplist.append(row)
    file.close()
    for row in tmplist:
        print(x,row)
        x = x + 1
    rowtodelete = int(input("Enter the row number to delete: "))
    del tmplist[rowtodelete]
    file = open("Salaries.csv","w")
    for row in tmplist:
        file.write(row)
    file.close()

tryagain = True
while tryagain == True:
    print("1) Add to file")
    print("2) View all records")
    print("3) Delete a record")
    print("4) Quit program")
    print()
    selection = input("Enter the number of your selection: ")
    if selection == "1":
        addtofile()
    elif selection == "2":
        viewrecords()
    elif selection == "3":
        deleterecord()
    elif selection == "4":
        tryagain = False
    else:
        print("Incorrect option")
```

Tkinter GUI

Graphical User Interface

Explanation

A **GUI** (graphical user interface) makes the program easier to use. It allows you, as the programmer, to create screens, text boxes and buttons to help the user navigate through the program in a more user-friendly way. **Tkinter** is a library of features in Python that allows you to do this.

Look at the code below and in particular the measurements that are used in the **window.geometry** and **button.place** lines.

```python
from tkinter import *

def Call():
        msg = Label(window, text = "You pressed the button")
        msg.place(x = 30, y = 50)
        button["bg"] = "blue"
        button["fg"] = "white"

window = Tk()
window.geometry("200x110")
button = Button(text = "Press me", command = Call)
button.place(x = 30, y = 20, width=120, height=25)
window.mainloop()
```

Now look at the window that this code will produce:

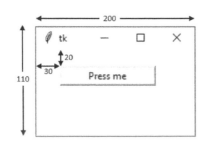

The **geometry** line in the code determines the size of the window and the **place** line in the code determines the position of the individual item on the window.

Once the button is pressed it will run the "Call" subprogram and change the window to look as follows:

Example Code

```
from tkinter import *
```
This line must go at the beginning of the program to import the Tkinter library.

```
window = Tk()
window.title("Window Title")
window.geometry("450x100")
```
Creates a window that will act as the display, referred to as "window", adds a title and defines the size of the window.

```
label = Label(text = "Enter number:")
```
Adds text to the screen displaying the message shown.

```
entry_box = Entry (text = 0)
```
Creates a blank entry box. Entry boxes can be used by the user to input data or used to display output.

```
output_box = Message(text = 0)
```
Creates a message box which is used to display an output.

```
output_box ["bg"] = "red"
```
Specifies the background colour of the object.

```
output_box ["fg"] = "white"
```
Specifies the font colour of the object.

```
output_box ["relief"] = "sunken"
```
Specifies the style of the box. This can be flat, raised, sunken, grooved and ridged.

```
list_box = Listbox()
```
Creates a drop-down list box which can only contain strings.

```
entry_box ["justify"] = "center"
```
Specifies the justification of the text in an entry box, but this does not work for message boxes.

```
button1 = Button(text = "Click here", command = click)
```
Creates a button that will run the subprogram "click".

```
label.place(x = 50, y = 20, width = 100, height = 25)
```
Specifies the position in which the object will appear in the window. If the position is not specified the item will not appear in the window.

```
entry_box.delete(0, END)
```
Deletes the contents of an entry or list box.

```
num = entry_box.get()
```
Saves the contents of an *entry box* and stores it in a variable called num. This does not work with message boxes.

```
answer = output_txt["text"]
```
Obtains the contents of a *message box* and stores it in a variable called answer. This does not work with an entry box.

```
output_txt["text"] = total
```
Changes the content of a message box to display the value of the variable total.

```
window.mainloop()
```
This must be at the end of the program to make sure it keeps working.

Every challenge you complete helps you become a better programmer.

Challenges

124

Create a window that will ask the user to enter their name. When they click on a button it should display the message "Hello" and their name and change the background colour and font colour of the message box.

125

Write a program that can be used instead of rolling a six-sided die in a board game. When the user clicks a button it should display a random whole number between 1 to 6 (inclusive).

126

Create a program that will ask the user to enter a number in a box. When they click on a button it will add that number to a total and display it in another box. This can be repeated as many times as they want and keep adding to the total. There should be another button that resets the total back to 0 and empties the original text box, ready for them to start again.

127

Create a window that will ask the user to enter a name in a text box. When they click on a button it will add it to the end of the list that is displayed on the screen. Create another button which will clear the list.

128

1 kilometre = 0.6214 miles and 1 mile = 1.6093 kilometres. Using these figures, make a program that will allow the user to convert between miles and kilometres.

129

Create a window that will ask the user to enter a number in a text box. When they click on a button it will use the code **`variable.isdigit()`** to check to see if it is a whole number. If it is a whole number, add it to a list box, otherwise clear the entry box. Add another button that will clear the list.

130

Alter program 129 to add a third button that will save the list to a .csv file. The code **`tmp_list = num_list.get(0,END)`** can be used to save the contents of a list box as a tuple called **`tmp_list`**.

131

Create a program that will allow the user to create a new .csv file. It should ask them to enter the name and age of a person and then allow them to add this to the end of the file they have just created.

132

Using the .csv file you created for the last challenge, create a program that will allow people to add names and ages to the list and create a button that will display the contents of the .csv file by importing it to a list box.

Answers

124

```
from tkinter import *

def click():
    name = textbox1.get()
    message = str("Hello " + name)
    textbox2["bg"] = "yellow"
    textbox2["fg"] = "blue"
    textbox2["text"] = message

window = Tk()
window.geometry("500x200")

label1 = Label(text = "Enter your name:")
label1.place(x = 30, y = 20)

textbox1 = Entry(text = "")
textbox1.place(x = 150, y = 20, width = 200, height = 25)
textbox1["justify"] = "center"
textbox1.focus()

button1 = Button(text = "Press me", command = click)
button1.place(x = 30, y = 50, width = 120, height = 25)

textbox2 = Message(text = "")
textbox2.place(x = 150, y = 50, width = 200, height = 25)
textbox2["bg"] = "white"
textbox2["fg"] = "black"

window.mainloop()
```

125

```python
from tkinter import *
import random

def click():
    num = random.randint(1,6)
    answer["text"] = num

window = Tk()
window.title("Roll a dice")
window.geometry("100x120")

button1 = Button(text = "Roll", command = click)
button1.place(x = 30, y = 30, width = 50, height = 25)

answer = Message(text = "")
answer.place(x = 40, y = 70, width = 30, height = 25)


window.mainloop()
```

126

```
from tkinter import *

def add_on():
    num = enter_txt.get()
    num = int(num)
    answer = output_txt["text"]
    answer = int(answer)
    total = num + answer
    output_txt["text"] = total

def reset():
    total = 0
    output_txt["text"] = 0
    enter_txt.delete(0, END)
    enter_txt.focus()

total = 0
num = 0

window = Tk()
window.title("Adding Together")
window.geometry("450x100")

enter_lbl = Label(text = "Enter a number:")
enter_lbl.place(x = 50, y = 20, width = 100, height = 25)

enter_txt = Entry(text = 0)
enter_txt.place(x = 150, y = 20, width = 100, height = 25)
enter_txt["justify"] = "center"
enter_txt.focus()

add_btn = Button(text = "Add", command = add_on)
add_btn.place(x = 300, y = 20, width = 50, height = 25)

output_lbl = Label(text = "Answer = ")
output_lbl.place(x = 50, y = 50, width = 100, height = 25)

output_txt = Message(text = 0)
output_txt.place(x = 150, y = 50, width = 100, height = 25)
output_txt["bg"] = "white"
output_txt["relief"] = "sunken"

clear_btn = Button(text = "Clear", command = reset)
clear_btn.place(x = 300, y = 50, width = 50, height = 25)

window.mainloop()
```

127

```python
from tkinter import *

def add_name():
    name = name_box.get()
    name_list.insert(END,name)
    name_box.delete(0, END)
    name_box.focus()

def clear_list():
    name_list.delete(0, END)
    name_box.focus()

window = Tk()
window.title("Names list")
window.geometry("400x200")


label1 = Label(text = "Enter a name:")
label1.place(x = 20, y = 20, width = 100, height = 25)

name_box = Entry(text = 0)
name_box.place(x = 120, y = 20, width = 100, height = 25)
name_box.focus()

button1 = Button(text = "Add to list", command = add_name)
button1.place(x = 250, y = 20, width = 100, height = 25)

name_list = Listbox()
name_list.place(x = 120, y = 50, width = 100, height = 100)

button2 = Button(text = "Clear list", command = clear_list)
button2.place(x = 250, y = 50, width = 100, height = 25)

window.mainloop()
```

128

```
def convert2():
    km = textbox1.get()
    km = int(km)
    message = km * 0.6214
    textbox2.delete(0, END)
    textbox2.insert(END, message)
    textbox2.insert(END, " miles")

window = Tk()
window.title("Distance")
window.geometry("260x200")

label1 = Label(text = "Enter the value you want to convert:")
label1.place(x = 30, y = 20)

textbox1 = Entry(text = "")
textbox1.place(x = 30, y = 50, width = 200, height = 25)
textbox1["justify"] = "center"
textbox1.focus()

convert1 = Button(text = "Convert miles to km", command = convert1)
convert1.place(x = 30, y = 80, width = 200, height = 25)

convert2 = Button(text = "Convert km to mile", command = convert2)
convert2.place(x = 30, y = 110, width = 200, height = 25)

textbox2 = Entry(text = "")
textbox2.place(x = 30, y = 140, width = 200, height = 25)
textbox2["justify"] = "center"

window.mainloop()
```

129

```python
from tkinter import *

def add_number():
    num = num_box.get()
    if num.isdigit():
        num_list.insert(END,num)
        num_box.delete(0, END)
        num_box.focus()
    else:
        num_box.delete(0, END)
        num_box.focus()

def clear_list():
    num_list.delete(0, END)
    num_box.focus()

window = Tk()
window.title("Number list")
window.geometry("400x200")

label1 = Label(text = "Enter a number:")
label1.place(x = 20, y = 20, width = 100, height = 25)

num_box = Entry(text = 0)
num_box.place(x = 120, y = 20, width = 100, height = 25)
num_box.focus()

button1 = Button(text = "Add to list", command = add_number)
button1.place(x = 250, y = 20, width = 100, height = 25)

num_list = Listbox()
num_list.place(x = 120, y = 50, width=100, height=100)

button2 = Button(text = "Clear list", command = clear_list)
button2.place(x = 250, y = 50, width = 100, height = 25)

window.mainloop()
```

130

```
from tkinter import *
import csv

def add_number():
    num = num_box.get()
    if num.isdigit():
        num_list.insert(END,num)
        num_box.delete(0, END)
        num_box.focus()
    else:
        num_box.delete(0, END)
        num_box.focus()

def clear_list():
    num_list.delete(0, END)
    num_box.focus()

def save_list():
    file = open("numbers.csv","w")
    tmp_list=num_list.get(0,END)
    item = 0
    for x in tmp_list:
        newrecord = tmp_list[item] + "\n"
        file.write(str(newrecord))
        item = item + 1
    file.close()

window = Tk()
window.title("Number list")
window.geometry("400x200")

label1 = Label(text = "Enter a number:")
label1.place(x = 20, y = 20, width = 100, height = 25)

num_box = Entry(text = 0)
num_box.place(x = 120, y = 20, width = 100, height = 25)
num_box.focus()

button1 = Button(text = "Add to list", command = add_number)
button1.place(x = 250, y = 20, width = 100, height = 25)

num_list = Listbox()
num_list.place(x = 120, y = 50, width = 100, height = 100)

button2 = Button(text = "Clear list", command = clear_list)
button2.place(x = 250, y = 50, width = 100, height = 25)

button3 = Button(text = "Save list", command = save_list)
button3.place(x = 250, y = 80, width = 100, height = 25)

window.mainloop()
```

131

```python
from tkinter import *
import csv

def create_new():
    file = open("ages.csv","w")
    file.close()

def save_list():
    file = open("ages.csv","a")
    name = name_box.get()
    age = age_box.get()
    newrecord = name + "," + age + "\n"
    file.write(str(newrecord))
    file.close()
    name_box.delete(0, END)
    age_box.delete(0, END)
    name_box.focus()

window = Tk()
window.title("People List")
window.geometry("400x100")

label1 = Label(text = "Enter a name:")
label1.place(x = 20, y = 20, width = 100, height = 25)

name_box = Entry(text = "")
name_box.place(x = 120, y = 20, width = 100, height = 25)
name_box["justify"]="left"
name_box.focus()

label2 = Label(text = "Enter their age:")
label2.place(x = 20, y = 50, width = 100, height = 25)

age_box = Entry(text = "")
age_box.place(x = 120, y = 50, width = 100, height = 25)
age_box["justify"] = "left"

button1 = Button(text = "Create new file", command = create_new)
button1.place(x = 250, y = 20, width = 100, height = 25)

button2 = Button(text = "Add to file", command = save_list)
button2.place(x = 250, y = 50, width = 100, height = 25)

window.mainloop()
```

132

```
from tkinter import *
import csv

def save_list():
    file = open("ages.csv","a")
    name = name_box.get()
    age = age_box.get()
    newrecord = name + "," + age + "\n"
    file.write(str(newrecord))
    file.close()
    name_box.delete(0, END)
    age_box.delete(0, END)
    name_box.focus()

def read_list():
    name_list.delete(0, END)
    file = list(csv.reader(open("ages.csv")))
    tmp=[]
    for row in file:
        tmp.append(row)
    x = 0
    for i in tmp:
        data = tmp[x]
        name_list.insert(END,data)
        x = x + 1

window = Tk()
window.title("People List")
window.geometry("400x200")


label1 = Label(text = "Enter a name:")
label1.place(x = 20, y = 20, width = 100, height = 25)

name_box = Entry(text = "")
name_box.place(x = 120, y = 20, width = 100, height = 25)
name_box["justify"] = "left"
name_box.focus()

label2 = Label(text = "Enter their age:")
label2.place(x = 20, y = 50, width = 100, height = 25)

age_box = Entry(text = "")
age_box.place(x = 120, y = 50, width = 100, height = 25)
age_box["justify"] = "left"

button1 = Button(text = "Add to file", command = save_list)
button1.place(x = 250, y = 20, width = 100, height = 25)

button2 = Button(text = "Read list", command = read_list)
button2.place(x = 250, y = 50, width = 100, height = 25)

label3 = Label(text = "Saved Names:")
label3.place(x = 20, y = 80, width = 100, height = 25)

name_list = Listbox()
name_list.place(x = 120, y = 80, width = 230, height = 100)

window.mainloop()
```

More Tkinter

Explanation

Here we will look at creating a **GUI** which includes more features and builds on the knowledge from the previous chapter.

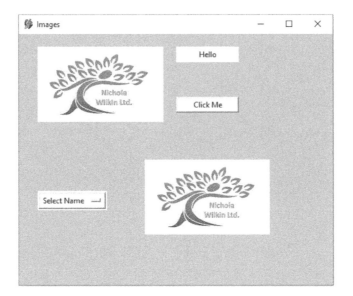

On this screen we have:

- changed the icon on the title bar;

- changed the background colour of the main window;

- added a static image of the logo to the top left, which will not change;

- created a label which, at the moment, displays "Hello";

- added a Click Me button;

- added a drop-down option entitled Select Name, which will display three names; "Bob", "Sue" and "Tim" to the user;

- added a second image in the lower half of the window which will change to show the photograph of the person selected from the drop-down list when the user clicks on the Click Me button.

You're creating some great programs.

All the code to create this window can be created using the code we looked at in the previous section and the example code you will be looking at in this chapter.

When using images in your program, it is easier if they are stored in the same folder as the program. Otherwise you need to include the entire dictionary location of the file as follows:

```
logo = PhotoImage(file="c:\\Python34\images\logo.gif")
```

If you store the image in the same folder as the program you only need to include the file name as shown below:

```
logo = PhotoImage(file="logo.gif")
```

Please note: it is only possible to use GIF or PGM/PPM file types for images in Tkinter as other file types are not supported. Make sure your images are saved in a suitable format and with a suitable name in the correct location before you start creating the programs, if at all possible, to make your life simpler.

Example Code

```
window.wm_iconbitmap("MyIcon.ico")
```
Changes the icon displayed in the title of the window.

```
window.configure(background = "light green")
```
Changes the background colour of the window, in this case to light green.

```
logo = PhotoImage(file = "logo.gif")
logoimage = Label(image = logo)
logoimage.place(x = 30, y = 20, width = 200, height = 120)
```
Displays an image in a label widget. This image will not change while the program is running.

```
photo = PhotoImage(file = "logo.gif")
photobox = Label(window, image = photo)
photobox.image = photo
photobox.place(x = 30, y = 20, width = 200, height = 120)
```
This is similar to the block above but as we want the image to change as we update the data we need to add the code **photobox.image = photo**, which makes it updatable.

```
selectName = StringVar(window)
selectName.set("Select Name")
namesList = OptionMenu(window,selectName,"Bob","Sue","Tim")
namesList.place(x = 30, y = 250)
```
Creates a variable called **selectName** which will store a string where the original value of the variable is "Select Name". It will then create a drop-down option menu which stores the value the user selects in the selectName variable and displays the values in the list: Bob, Sue and Tim.

```
def clicked():
 sel = selectName.get()
 mesg = "Hello " + sel
 mlabel["text"] = mesg
 if sel == "Bob":
  photo = PhotoImage(file = "Bob.gif")
  photobox.image = photo
 elif sel == "Sue":
  photo = PhotoImage(file = "Sue.gif")
  photobox.image = photo
 elif sel == "Tim":
  photo = PhotoImage(file = "Tim.gif")
  photobox.image = photo
 else:
  photo = PhotoImage(file = "logo.gif")
  photobox.image = photo
 photobox["image"] = photo
 photobox.update()
```

In this example, when a button is clicked it will run the "clicked" subprogram. This will obtain the value from the selectName variable and create a message that will be displayed in a label. It will then check to see which option has been selected and change the picture to the correct image, which is displayed in the photo variable. If no name is selected it will simply show the logo.

Don't forget, if you get stuck, look at some of your earlier programs, they may help you.

Challenges

133

Create your own icon that consists of several vertical multi-coloured lines. Create a logo which measures 200 x 150, using Paint or another graphics package. Create the following window using your own icon and logo.

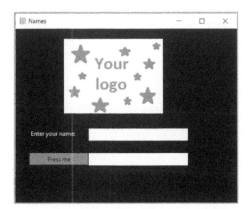

When the user enters their name and clicks on the Press Me button it should display "Hello" and their name in the second text box.

136

Create a program that will ask the user to enter a name and then select the gender for that person from a drop-down list. It should then add the name and the gender (separated by a comma) to a list box when the user clicks on a button.

134

Create a new program that will generate two random whole numbers between 10 and 50. It should ask the user to add the numbers together and type in the answer. If they get the question correct, display a suitable image such as a tick; if they get the answer wrong, display another suitable image such as a cross. They should click on a Next button to get another question.

135

Create a simple program that shows a drop-down list containing several colours and a Click Me button. When the user selects a colour from the list and clicks the button it should change the background of the window to that colour. For an extra challenge, try to avoid using an if statement to do this.

137

Change program 136 so that when a new name and gender is added to the list box it is also written to a text file. Add another button that will display the entire text file in the main Python shell window.

138

Save several images in the same folder as your program and call them 1.gif, 2.gif, 3.gif, etc. Make sure they are all .gif files. Display one in a window and ask the user to enter a number. It should then use that number to choose the correct file name and display the correct image.

Answers

133

```python
from tkinter import *

def click():
    name = textbox1.get()
    message = str("Hello " + name)
    textbox2["text"] = message

window = Tk()
window.title("Names")
window.geometry("450x350")
window.wm_iconbitmap("stripes.ico")
window.configure(background = "black")

logo = PhotoImage(file = "Mylogo.gif")
logoimage = Label(image = logo)
logoimage.place(x = 100, y = 20, width = 200, height = 150)

label1 = Label(text = "Enter your name:")
label1.place(x = 30, y = 200)
label1["bg"] = "black"
label1["fg"] = "white"

textbox1 = Entry(text = "")
textbox1.place(x = 150, y = 200, width = 200, height = 25)
textbox1["justify"] = "center"
textbox1.focus()

button1 = Button(text = "Press me", command = click)
button1.place(x = 30, y = 250, width = 120, height = 25)
button1["bg"] = "yellow"

textbox2 = Message(text = "")
textbox2.place(x = 150, y = 250, width = 200, height = 25)
textbox2["bg"] = "white"
textbox2["fg"] = "black"

window.mainloop()
```

134

```python
from tkinter import *
import random

def checkans():
    theirans = ansbox.get()
    theirans = int(theirans)
    num1 = num1box["text"]
    num1 = int(num1)
    num2 = num2box["text"]
    num2 = int(num2)
    ans = num1 + num2
    if theirans == ans:
        img = PhotoImage(file = "correct.gif")
        imgbx.image = img
    else:
        img = PhotoImage(file = "wrong.gif")
        imgbx.image = img
    imgbx["image"] = img
    imgbx.update()

def nextquestion():
    ansbox.delete(0,END)
    num1 = random.randint(10,50)
    num1box["text"] = num1
    num2 = random.randint(10,50)
    num2box["text"] = num2
    img = PhotoImage(file = "")
    imgbx.image = img
    imgbx["image"] = img
    imgbx.update()

window = Tk()
window.title("Addition")
window.geometry("250x300")

num1box = Label(text = "0")
num1box.place(x = 50, y = 30, width = 25, height = 25)
addsymbl = Message(text = "+")
addsymbl.place(x = 75, y = 30, width = 25, height = 25)
num2box = Label(text = "0")
num2box.place(x = 100, y = 30, width = 25, height = 25)
eqlsymbl = Message(text = "=")
eqlsymbl.place(x = 125, y = 30, width = 25, height = 25)
ansbox = Entry(text = "")
ansbox.place(x = 150, y = 30, width = 25, height = 25)
ansbox["justify"] = "center"
ansbox.focus()
checkbtn = Button(text = "Check", command = checkans)
checkbtn.place(x = 50, y = 60, width = 75, height = 25)
nextbtn = Button(text = "Next", command = nextquestion)
nextbtn.place(x = 130, y = 60, width= 75, height = 25)
img = PhotoImage(file = "")
imgbx = Label(image = img)
imgbx.image = img
imgbx.place(x = 25, y = 100, width = 200, height = 150)

nextquestion()

window.mainloop()
```

135

```
from tkinter import *

def clicked():
    sel = selectcolour.get()
    window.configure(background = sel)

window = Tk()
window.title("background")
window.geometry("200x200")

selectcolour = StringVar(window)
selectcolour.set("Grey")

colourlist = OptionMenu(window, selectcolour, "Grey","Red","Blue","Green","Yellow")
colourlist.place(x = 50, y = 30)

clickme = Button(text = "Click Me", command = clicked)
clickme.place(x = 50, y = 150, width = 60, height = 30)

mainloop()
```

136

```
from tkinter import *

def add_to_list():
    name = namebox.get()
    namebox.delete(0,END)
    genderselection = gender.get()
    gender.set("M/F")
    newdata = name + ", " + genderselection + "\n"
    name_list.insert(END,newdata)
    namebox.focus()

window = Tk()
window.title("People List")
window.geometry("400x400")

namelbl = Label(text = "Enter their name:")
namelbl.place(x = 50, y = 50, width = 100, height = 25)
namebox = Entry(text = "")
namebox.place(x = 150, y = 50, width = 150, height = 25)
namebox.focus()

genderlbl = Label(text = "Select Gender")
genderlbl.place(x = 50, y = 100, width = 100, height = 25)
gender = StringVar(window)
gender.set("M/F")
gendermenu = OptionMenu(window, gender, "M","F")
gendermenu.place(x = 150, y = 100)

name_list = Listbox()
name_list.place(x = 150, y = 150, width = 150, height = 100)

addbtn = Button(text = "Add to List", command = add_to_list)
addbtn.place(x = 50, y = 300, width = 100, height = 25)

window.mainloop()
```

137

```
from tkinter import *

def add_to_list():
    name = namebox.get()
    namebox.delete(0,END)
    genderselection = gender.get()
    gender.set("M/F")
    newdata = name + ", " + genderselection + "\n"
    name_list.insert(END,newdata)
    namebox.focus()
    file = open("names.txt","a")
    file.write(newdata)
    file.close()

def print_list():
    file = open("names.txt","r")
    print(file.read())

window = Tk()
window.title("People List")
window.geometry("400x400")

namelbl = Label(text = "Enter their name:")
namelbl.place(x = 50, y = 50, width = 100, height = 25)
namebox = Entry(text = "")
namebox.place(x = 150, y = 50, width = 150, height = 25)
namebox.focus()

genderlbl = Label(text = "Select Gender")
genderlbl.place(x = 50, y = 100, width = 100, height = 25)
gender = StringVar(window)
gender.set("M/F")
gendermenu = OptionMenu(window, gender, "M","F")
gendermenu.place(x = 150, y = 100)

name_list = Listbox()
name_list.place(x = 150, y = 150, width = 150, height = 100)

addbtn = Button(text = "Add to List", command = add_to_list)
addbtn.place(x = 50, y = 300, width = 100, height = 25)

printlst = Button(text = "Print List", command = print_list)
printlst.place(x = 175, y = 300, width = 100, height = 25)

window.mainloop()
```

138

```
from tkinter import *

def clicked():
    num = selection.get()
    artref = num + ".gif"
    photo = PhotoImage(file = artref)
    photobox.image = photo
    photobox["image"] = photo
    photobox.update()

window = Tk()
window.title("Art")
window.geometry("400x350")

art = PhotoImage(file = "1.gif")
photobox = Label(window,image = art)
photobox.image = art
photobox.place(x = 100, y = 20, width = 200, height = 150)

label = Label(text = "Select Art number:")
label.place(x = 50, y = 200, width = 100, height = 25)

selection = Entry(text = "")
selection.place(x = 200, y = 200, width = 100, height = 25)
selection.focus()

button = Button(text = "See Art", command = clicked)
button.place(x = 150, y = 250, width = 100, height = 25)

window.mainloop()
```

SQLite

Explanation

SQL stands for "Structured Query Language" and is the main language that the large database packages use. **SQLite** is free software that can be used as an SQL database. You can download the latest version of the software from **www.sqlite.org**.

From the download page you need to select one of the "Precompiled Binaries" options for either Mac OS or Windows that includes the "command-line-shell".

To use SQL you need to load the "DB Browser for SQLite" which you can download from **https://sqlitebrowser.org.**

Understanding a Relational Database

We will use the example of a small manufacturing company that stores the details of their employees in an **SQL** database.

Below is an example of the Employees table, which contains the details of all the employees in the company. The contents of a table can be viewed by clicking on the Browse Data tab.

Table: Employees ▼

	ID	Name	Dept	Salary
	Filter	Filter	Filter	Filter
1	1	Bob	Sales	25000
2	2	Sue	IT	28500
3	3	Tim	Sales	25000
4	4	Anne	Admin	18500
5	5	Paul	IT	28500
6	6	Simon	Sales	22000
7	7	Karen	Manufacturing	18500
8	8	Mark	Manufacturing	19000
9	9	George	Manufacturing	18500
10	10	Keith	Manufacturing	15000

It has four fields (ID, Name, Dept and Salary) and 10 records in it (one for each employee). Take a look at the employees list and you will notice that more than one employee is listed in the same department. In most databases you would find repetitive data such as this. To make the database work more efficiently the repeated data are often stored in a separate table. In this case there is a department table which would store all the information about each department to save having to repeat all the department details for each employee.

Here we can see the Departments table holding the details about each department. We have simplified it and only include one piece of data for each department (in this case the manager's name) but it will still save having to input the manager's name on every record, which we would have to do if the data were all being saved in one large table.

By splitting the data into two tables like this, if we need to update the manager it only needs to be updated in one place rather than updating it several times, which we would need to do if it was all stored in a single table.

This is known as a **one-to-many** relationship as one department can have many employees in it.

 A **primary key** is the field (usually the first one) in each table that stores the unique identifier for that record. Therefore, in the Employees table the primary key will be the ID column and in the Department table the primary key will be Dept.

When creating a table, you need to identify the following for each field:

- the name of the field (field names cannot contain spaces and must follow the same rules as variable names);

- if it is a primary key;

- the data type for that field.

The data types you can use are as follows:

- **integer**: the value is an integer value;

- **real**: the value is a floating-point value;

- **text**: the value is a text string;

- **blob**: the value is stored exactly as it was input.

You can also specify if the field cannot be left blank by adding **NOT NULL** to the end of the field when you create it.

Example Code

```
import sqlite3
```
This must be the first line of the program to allow Python to use the SQLite3 library.

```
with sqlite3.connect("company.db") as db:
  cursor=db.cursor()
```
Connects to the company database. If no such database exists, it will create one. The file will be stored in the same folder as the program.

```
cursor.execute("""CREATE TABLE IF NOT EXISTS employees(
  id integer PRIMARY KEY,
  name text NOT NULL,
  dept text NOT NULL,
  salary integer);""")
```
Creates a table called employees which has four fields (id, name, dept and salary). It specifies the data type for each field, defines which field is the primary key and which fields cannot be left blank. The triple speech marks allow the code to be split over several lines to make it easier to read rather than having it all displayed in one line.

```
cursor.execute("""INSERT INTO employees(id,name,dept,salary)
  VALUES("1","Bob","Sales","25000")""")
db.commit()
```
Inserts data into the employees table. The **db.commit()** line saves the changes.

```
newID = input("Enter ID number: ")
newame = input("Enter name: ")
newDept = input("Enter department: ")
newSalary = input("Enter salary: ")
cursor.execute("""INSERT INTO employees(id,name,dept,salary)
  VALUES(?,?,?,?)""",(newID,newName,newDept,newSalary))
db.commit()
```
Allows a user to enter new data which is then inserted into the table.

```
cursor.execute("SELECT * FROM employees")
print(cursor.fetchall())
```
Displays all the data from the employees table.

```
db.close()
```
This must be the last line in the program to close the database.

```
cursor.execute("SELECT * FROM employees")
for x in cursor.fetchall():
 print(x)
```
Displays all the data from the employees table and displays each record on a separate line.

```
cursor.execute("SELECT * FROM employees ORDER BY name")
for x in cursor.fetchall():
 print(x)
```
Selects all the data from the employees table, sorted by name, and displays each record on a separate line.

```
cursor.execute("SELECT * FROM employees WHERE salary>20000")
```
Selects all the data from the employees table where the salary is over 20,000.

```
cursor.execute("SELECT * FROM employees WHERE dept='Sales'")
```
Selects all the data from the employees table where the department is "Sales".

```
cursor.execute("""SELECT employees.id,employees.name,dept.manager
 FROM employees,dept WHERE employees.dept=dept.dept
 AND employees.salary >20000""")
```
Selects the ID and name fields from the employees table and the manager field from the department table if the salary is over 20,000.

```
cursor.execute("SELECT id,name,salary FROM employees")
```
Selects the ID, name and salary fields from the employees table.

```
whichDept = input("Enter a department: ")
cursor.execute("SELECT * FROM employees WHERE dept=?",[whichDept])
for x in cursor.fetchall():
 print(x)
```
Allows the user to type in a department and displays the records of all the employees in that department.

```
cursor.execute("""SELECT employees.id,employees.name,dept.manager
 FROM employees,dept WHERE employees.dept=dept.dept""")
```
Selects the ID and name fields from the employees table and the manager field from the department table, using the dept fields to link the data. If you do not specify how the tables are linked, Python will assume every employee works in every department and you will not get the results you are expecting.

```
cursor.execute("UPDATE employees SET name = 'Tony' WHERE id=1")
db.commit()
```
Updates the data in the table (overwriting the original data) to change the name to "Tony" for employee ID 1.

```
cursor.execute("DELETE employees WHERE id=1")
```

Challenges

139

Create an SQL database called PhoneBook that contains a table called Names with the following data:

ID	First Name	Surname	Phone Number
1	Simon	Howels	01223 349752
2	Karen	Phillips	01954 295773
3	Darren	Smith	01583 749012
4	Anne	Jones	01323 567322
5	Mark	Smith	01223 855534

141

Create a new SQL database called BookInfo that will store a list of authors and the books they wrote.
It will have two tables. The first one should be called Authors and contain the following data:

Name	Place of Birth
Agatha Christie	Torquay
Cecelia Ahern	Dublin
J.K. Rowling	Bristol
Oscar Wilde	Dublin

The second should be called Books and contain the following data:

ID	Title	Author	Date Published
1	De Profundis	Oscar Wilde	1905
2	Harry Potter and the chamber of secrets	J.K. Rowling	1998
3	Harry Potter and the prisoner of Azkaban	J.K. Rowling	1999
4	Lyrebird	Cecelia Ahern	2017
5	Murder on the Orient Express	Agatha Christie	1934
6	Perfect	Cecelia Ahern	2017
7	The marble collector	Cecelia Ahern	2016
8	The murder on the links	Agatha Christie	1923
9	The picture of Dorian Gray	Oscar Wilde	1890
10	The secret adversary	Agatha Christie	1921
11	The seven dials mystery	Agatha Christie	1929
12	The year I met you	Cecelia Ahern	2014

140

Using the PhoneBook database from program 139, write a program that will display the following menu.

```
Main Menu

1) View phone book
2) Add to phone book
3) Search for surname
4) Delete person from phone book
5) Quit

Enter your selection:
```

If the user selects 1, they should be able to view the entire phonebook. If they select 2, it should allow them to add a new person to the phonebook. If they select 3, it should ask them for a surname and then display only the records of people with the same surname. If they select 4, it should ask for an ID and then delete that record from the table. If they select 5, it should end the program. Finally, it should display a suitable message if they enter an incorrect selection from the menu. They should return to the menu after each action, until they select 5.

142

Using the BookInfo database from program 141, display the list of authors and their place of birth. Ask the user to enter a place of birth and then show the title, date published and author's name for all the books by authors who were born in the location they selected.

143

Using the BookInfo database, ask the user to enter a year and display all the books published after that year, sorted by the year they were published.

144

Using the BookInfo database, ask the user for an author's name and then save all the books by that author to a text file, with each field separated by dashes so it looks as follows:

```
5 - Murder on the Orient Express - Agatha Christie - 1934
8 - The murder on the links - Agatha Christie - 1923
10 - The secret adversary - Agatha Christie - 1921
11 - The seven dials mystery - Agatha Christie - 1929
```

Open the text file to make sure it has worked correctly.

You have learnt so much. Look back on all the challenges and programming techniques you have learnt. It really is amazing.

145

Create a program that displays the following screen:

It should save the data to an SQL database called TestScores when the Add button is clicked. The Clear button should clear the window.

Answers

139

```python
import sqlite3

with sqlite3.connect("PhoneBook.db") as db:
    cursor = db.cursor()

cursor.execute(""" CREATE TABLE IF NOT EXISTS Names(
id integer PRIMARY KEY,
 firstname text,
 surname text,
 phonenumber text); """)

cursor.execute(""" INSERT INTO Names(id,firstname,surname,phonenumber)
VALUES("1","Simon","Howels","01223 349752")""")
db.commit()

cursor.execute(""" INSERT INTO Names(id,firstname,surname,phonenumber)
VALUES("2","Karen","Phillips","01954 295773")""")
db.commit()

cursor.execute(""" INSERT INTO Names(id,firstname,surname,phonenumber)
VALUES("3","Darren","Smith","01583 749012")""")
db.commit()

cursor.execute(""" INSERT INTO Names(id,firstname,surname,phonenumber)
VALUES("4","Anne","Jones","01323 567322")""")
db.commit()

cursor.execute(""" INSERT INTO Names(id,firstname,surname,phonenumber)
VALUES("5","Mark","Smith","01223 855534")""")
db.commit()

db.close()
```

140

```python
import sqlite3

def viewphonebook():
    cursor.execute("SELECT * FROM Names")
    for x in cursor.fetchall():
        print(x)

def addtophonebook():
    newid = int(input("Enter ID: "))
    newfname = input("Enter first name: ")
    newsname = input("Enter surname: ")
    newpnum = input("Enter phone number: ")
    cursor.execute("""INSERT INTO Names (id,firstname,surname,phonenumber)
VALUES (?,?,?,?)""", (newid,newfname,newsname,newpnum))
    db.commit()

def selectname():
    selectsurname = input("Enter a surname: ")
    cursor.execute("SELECT * FROM Names WHERE surname = ?", [selectsurname])
    for x in cursor.fetchall():
        print(x)

def deletedata():
    selectid = int(input("Enter ID: "))
    cursor.execute("DELETE FROM Names WHERE id = ?", [selectid])
    cursor.execute("SELECT * FROM Names")
    for x in cursor.fetchall():
        print(x)
    db.commit()

with sqlite3.connect("PhoneBook.db") as db:
    cursor = db.cursor()

def main():
    again = "y"
    while again == "y":
        print()
        print("Main Menu")
        print()
        print("1) View phone book")
        print("2) Add to phone book")
        print("3) Search for surname")
        print("4) Delete person from phone book")
        print("5) Quit")
        print()
        selection = int(input("Enter your selection: "))
        print()

        if selection == 1:
            viewphonebook()
        elif selection == 2:
            addtophonebook()
        elif selection == 3:
            selectname()
        elif selection == 4:
            deletedata()
        elif selection == 5:
            again = "n"
        else:
            print("Incorrect selection entered")

main()
db.close()
```

141

```python
import sqlite3

with sqlite3.connect("BookInfo.db") as db:
    cursor = db.cursor()

cursor.execute(""" CREATE TABLE IF NOT EXISTS Authors(
Name text PRIMARY KEY,
PlaceofBirth text); """)

cursor.execute(""" INSERT INTO Authors(Name,PlaceofBirth)
VALUES("Agatha Christie","Torquay")""")
db.commit()

cursor.execute(""" INSERT INTO Authors(Name,PlaceofBirth)
VALUES("Cecelia Ahern","Dublin")""")
db.commit()
cursor.execute(""" INSERT INTO Authors(Name,PlaceofBirth)
VALUES("J.K. Rowling","Bristol")""")
db.commit()
cursor.execute(""" INSERT INTO Authors(Name,PlaceofBirth)
VALUES("Oscar Wilde","Dublin")""")
db.commit()

cursor.execute(""" CREATE TABLE IF NOT EXISTS Books(
ID integer PRIMARY KEY,
Title text,
Author text,
DatePublished integer); """)

cursor.execute(""" INSERT INTO Books(ID,Title,Author,DatePublished)
VALUES("1","De Profundis","Oscar Wilde","1905")""")
db.commit()
cursor.execute(""" INSERT INTO Books(ID,Title,Author,DatePublished)
VALUES("2","Harry Potter and the chamber of secrets","J.K. Rowling","1998")""")
db.commit()
cursor.execute(""" INSERT INTO Books(ID,Title,Author,DatePublished)
VALUES("3","Harry Potter and the prisoner of Azkaban","J.K. Rowling","1999")""")
db.commit()
cursor.execute(""" INSERT INTO Books(ID,Title,Author,DatePublished)
VALUES("4","Lyrebird","Cecelia Ahern","2017")""")
db.commit()
cursor.execute(""" INSERT INTO Books(ID,Title,Author,DatePublished)
VALUES("5","Murder on the Orient Express","Agatha Christie","1934")""")
db.commit()
cursor.execute(""" INSERT INTO Books(ID,Title,Author,DatePublished)
VALUES("6","Perfect","Cecelia Ahern","2017")""")
db.commit()
cursor.execute(""" INSERT INTO Books(ID,Title,Author,DatePublished)
VALUES("7","The marble collector","Cecelia Ahern","2016")""")
db.commit()
cursor.execute(""" INSERT INTO Books(ID,Title,Author,DatePublished)
VALUES("8","The murder on the links","Agatha Christie","1923")""")
db.commit()
cursor.execute(""" INSERT INTO Books(ID,Title,Author,DatePublished)
VALUES("9","The picture of Dorian Gray","Oscar Wilde","1890")""")
db.commit()
cursor.execute(""" INSERT INTO Books(ID,Title,Author,DatePublished)
VALUES("10","The secret adversary","Agatha Christie","1921")""")
db.commit()
cursor.execute(""" INSERT INTO Books(ID,Title,Author,DatePublished)
VALUES("11","The seven dials mystery","Agatha Christie","1929")""")
db.commit()
cursor.execute(""" INSERT INTO Books(ID,Title,Author,DatePublished)
VALUES("12","The year I met you","Cecelia Ahern","2014")""")
db.commit()

db.close()
```

142

```python
import sqlite3

with sqlite3.connect("BookInfo.db") as db:
    cursor = db.cursor()

cursor.execute("SELECT * FROM Authors")
for x in cursor.fetchall():
        print(x)

print()
location = input("Enter a place of birth: ")
print()

cursor.execute("""SELECT  Books.Title, Books.DatePublished, Books.Author
FROM Books,Authors WHERE Authors.Name=Books.Author AND Authors.PlaceofBirth=?""",[location])
for x in cursor.fetchall():
    print(x)

db.close()
```

143

```python
import sqlite3

with sqlite3.connect("BookInfo.db") as db:
    cursor = db.cursor()

selectionyear = int(input("Enter a year: "))
print()

cursor.execute("""SELECT  Books.Title, Books.DatePublished, Books.Author
FROM Books WHERE DatePublished>? ORDER BY DatePublished""",[selectionyear])
for x in cursor.fetchall():
    print(x)

db.close()
```

144

```python
import sqlite3

file = open("BooksList.txt","w")

with sqlite3.connect("BookInfo.db") as db:
    cursor = db.cursor()

cursor.execute("SELECT Name from Authors")
for x in cursor.fetchall():
    print(x)

print()
selectauthor = input("Enter an author's name. ")
print()

cursor.execute("SELECT *FROM Books WHERE Author=?",[selectauthor])
for x in cursor.fetchall():
    newrecord = str(x[0]) + " - " + x[1] + " - " + x[2] + " - " + str(x[3]) + "\n"
    file.write(newrecord)

file.close()

db.close()
```

145

```python
import sqlite3
from tkinter import *

def addtolist():
    newname = sname.get()
    newgrade = sgrade.get()
    cursor.execute("""INSERT INTO Scores (name,score)
VALUES (?,?)""",(newname,newgrade))
    db.commit()
    sname.delete(0,END)
    sgrade.delete(0,END)
    sname.focus()

def clearlist():
    sname.delete(0,END)
    sgrade.delete(0,END)
    sname.focus()

with sqlite3.connect("TestScore.db") as db:
    cursor = db.cursor()

cursor.execute(""" CREATE TABLE IF NOT EXISTS Scores(
id integer PRIMARY KEY, name text, score integer); """)

window = Tk()
window.title("TestScores")
window.geometry("450x200")

label1 = Label(text = "Enter student's name:")
label1.place(x = 30, y = 35)
sname = Entry(text = "")
sname.place(x = 150, y = 35, width = 200, height = 25)
sname.focus()
label2 = Label(text = "Enter student's grade:")
label2.place(x = 30, y = 80)
sgrade = Entry(text = "")
sgrade.place(x = 150, y = 80, width = 200, height = 25)
sgrade.focus()
addbtn = Button(text = "Add", command = addtolist )
addbtn.place(x = 150, y = 120, width = 75, height = 25)
clearbtn = Button(text = "Clear", command = clearlist)
clearbtn.place(x = 250, y = 120, width = 75, height = 25)

window.mainloop()
db.close()
```

Part 11

Chunky Challenges

Introduction to Part II

In this section, you are given some large programming challenges to work through. These will take longer than the previous challenges and you are likely to have to refer to earlier sections of the book to remind yourself of some of the key skills you have covered. Don't feel bad if you need to look up key lines of code in previous sections; even experienced programmers get help when they come across a tricky piece of code with which they are not familiar. It is all part of the learning process and is exactly how this book was written to be used.

Each challenge contains a list of the skills that will be needed so you can decide if you feel ready to attempt the challenge. It also includes a description of the challenge and a section outlining problems you will have to overcome. The solutions in this section are much larger and some are split over several pages, but should be read as a continuous single program for that challenge. If a program does need to be split across separate pages we try to split it between the subprograms or in a natural break if possible.

Read each challenge all the way through before attempting it so you are aware of the pitfalls. Once you have read through the challenge, sit back and have a think about how you are going to approach it. You may want to scribble some notes, or if you are feeling very keen and know how, you may even venture into writing a flow chart. There is no point in diving straight into tapping out lines of code with no idea where you are heading, as you are likely to get into a muddle and may lose faith in your abilities. Make a plan, split the large problem into small, manageable chunks, and then tackle each chunk, testing each section as you go. Now, make yourself a drink, grab a notebook and pencil, take a deep breath, turn the page and have a go at the first one.

146: Shift Code

In this challenge you will need to use the following skills:

- input and display data;
- lists;
- splitting and joining strings;
- if statements;
- loops (while and for);
- subprograms.

The Challenge

A shift code is where a message can be easily encoded and is one of the simplest codes to use. Each letter is moved forwards through the alphabet a set number of letters to be represented by a new letter. For instance, "abc" becomes "bcd" when the code is shifted by one (i.e. each letter in the alphabet is moved forward one character).

You need to create a program which will display the following menu:

```
1) Make a code
2) Decode a message
3) Quit

Enter your selection:
```

If the user selects 1, they should be able to type in a message (including spaces) and then enter a number. Python should then display the encoded message once the shift code has been applied.

If the user selects 2, they should enter an encoded message and the correct number and it should display the decoded message (i.e. move the correct number of letters backwards through the alphabet).

If they select 3 it should stop the program from running.

After they have encoded or decoded a message the menu should be displayed to them again until they select quit.

Problems You Will Have to Overcome

Decide if you want to allow both upper and lower case letters or if you want to convert all the data into one case.

Decide if you are allowing punctuation.

If the shift makes the letter go past the end of the alphabet it should start again; i.e. if the user enters "xyz" and 5 is entered as the shift number, it should display "bcd". This should work the opposite way for decoding a message, so if the value gets to "a" it will go back to "w".

Make sure that suitable messages are displayed if the user selects an inappropriate option on the menu or selects an inappropriate number to make the shift code.

Test out your decode option by decoding the message "we ovugjohsslunl", which was created with the number 7 when the code only uses "abcdefghijklmnopqrstuvwxyz " (note the space at the end).

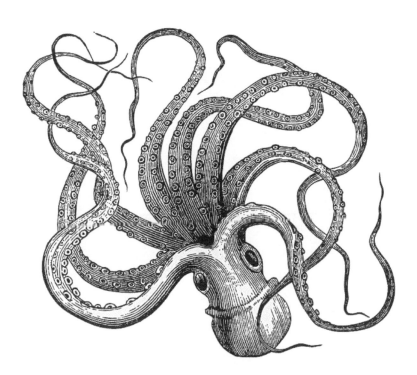

Answer

```python
alphabet = ["a","b","c","d","e","f","g","h","i","j",
            "k","l","m","n","o","p","q","r","s","t",
            "u","v","w","x","y","z"," "]

def get_data():
    word = input("Enter your message: ")
    word = word.lower()
    num = int(input("Enter a number (1-26): "))
    if num > 26 or num == 0:
        while num > 26 or num == 0:
            num = int(input("Out of range, please enter a number (1-26): "))
    data = (word,num)
    return(data)

def make_code(word,num):
    new_word = ""
    for x in word:
        y = alphabet.index(x)
        y = y + num
        if y > 26:
            y = y - 27
        char = alphabet[y]
        new_word = new_word + char
    print(new_word)
    print()

def decode(word,num):
    new_word = ""
    for x in word:
        y = alphabet.index(x)
        y = y - num
        if y < 0:
            y = y + 27
        char = alphabet[y]
        new_word = new_word+char
    print(new_word)
    print()


def main():
    again = True
    while again == True:
        print("1) Make a code")
        print("2) Decode a message")
        print("3) Quit")
        print()
        selection = int(input("Enter your selection: "))
        if selection == 1:
            (word,num) = get_data()
            make_code(word,num)
        elif selection == 2:
            (word,num) = get_data()
            decode(word,num)
        elif selection == 3:
            again = False
        else:
            print("Incorrect selection")

main()
```

147: Mastermind

In this challenge you will need to use the following skills:

- input and display data;
- lists;
- random choice from a list;
- if statements;
- loops (while and for);
- subprograms.

The Challenge

You are going to make an on-screen version of the board game "Mastermind". The computer will automatically generate four colours from a list of possible colours (it should be possible for the computer to randomly select the same colour more than once). For instance, the computer may choose "red", "blue", "red", "green". This sequence should **not** be displayed to the user.

After this is done the user should enter their choice of four colours from the same list the computer used. For instance, they may choose "pink", "blue", "yellow" and "red".

After the user has made their selection, the program should display how many colours they got right in the correct position and how many colours they got right but in the wrong position. In the example above, it should display the message "Correct colour in the correct place: 1" and "Correct colour but in the wrong place: 1".

The user continues guessing until they correctly enter the four colours in the order they should be in. At the end of the game it should display a suitable message and tell them how many guesses they took.

Problems You Will Have to Overcome

The hardest part of this game is working out the logic for checking how many the user has correct and how many are in the wrong place. Using the example above, if the user enters "blue", "blue", "blue", "blue" they should see the messages, "Correct colour in the correct place: 1" and "Correct colour but in the wrong place: 0".

Decide if there is an easier way of allowing the user to enter their selection (e.g. using a code or a single letter to represent the colour). If using the first letter, make sure you only use colours that have a unique first letter (i.e. avoid using blue, black and brown as options and select just one of these as a possibility). Make your instructions clear to the user.

Decide if you want to allow upper and lower case or if it is easier to convert everything to the same case.

Make sure you build in validation checks to make sure the user is only entering valid data and display a suitable message if they make an incorrect selection. If they do make an incorrect selection you may want to allow them to enter the data again, rather than class it as an incorrect guess.

Answer

```python
import random

def select_col():
    colours = ["r","b","o","y","p","g","w"]
    c1 = random.choice(colours)
    c2 = random.choice(colours)
    c3 = random.choice(colours)
    c4 = random.choice(colours)
    data = (c1,c2,c3,c4)
    return data

def tryit(c1,c2,c3,c4):
    print("The colours are: (r)ed, (b)lue, (o)range, (y)ellow, (p)ink, (g)reen and (w)hite.")
    try_again = True
    while try_again == True:
        u1 = input("Enter your choice for place 1: ")
        u1 = u1.lower()
        if u1 != "r" and u1 != "b" and u1 != "o" and u1 != "y" and u1 != "p" and u1 != "g" and u1 != "w":
            print("Incorrect selection")
        else:
            try_again = False
    try_again = True
    while try_again == True:
        u2 = input("Enter your choice for place 2: ")
        u2 = u2.lower()
        if u2 != "r" and u2 != "b" and u2 != "o" and u2 != "y" and u2 != "p" and u2 != "g" and u2 != "w":
            print("Incorrect selection")
        else:
            try_again = False
    try_again = True
    while try_again == True:
        u3 = input("Enter your choice for place 3: ")
        u3 = u3.lower()
        if u3 != "r" and u3 != "b" and u3 != "o" and u3 != "y" and u3 != "p" and u3 != "g" and u3 != "w":
            print("Incorrect selection")
        else:
            try_again = False
    try_again = True
    while try_again == True:
        u4 = input("Enter your choice for place 4: ")
        u4 = u4.lower()
        if u4 != "r" and u4 != "b" and u4 != "o" and u4 != "y" and u4 != "p" and u4 != "g" and u4 != "w":
            print("Incorrect selection")
        else:
            try_again = False
    correct = 0
    wrong_place = 0
    if c1 == u1:
        correct = correct + 1
    elif c1 == u2 or c1 == u3 or c1 == u4:
        wrong_place = wrong_place + 1
    if c2 == u2:
        correct = correct + 1
    elif c2 == u1 or c2 == u3 or c2 == u4:
        wrong_place = wrong_place + 1
    if u3 == c3:
        correct = correct + 1
    elif c3 == u1 or c3 == u2 or c3 == u4:
        wrong_place = wrong_place + 1
    if u4 == c4:
        correct = correct + 1
    elif c4 == u1 or c4 == u2 or c4 == u3:
        wrong_place = wrong_place + 1
    print("Correct colour in the correct place: ",correct)
    print("Correct colour but in the wrong place: ",wrong_place)
    print()
    data2 = [correct,wrong_place]
    return data2

def main():
    (c1,c2,c3,c4) = select_col()
    score = 0
    play = True
    while play == True:
        (correct,wrong_place) = tryit(c1,c2,c3,c4)
        score = score + 1
        if correct == 4:
            play = False
    print("You win!")
    print("You took", score,"guesses")

main()
```

148: Passwords

In this challenge you will need to use the following skills:

- input and display data;

- lists;

- if statements;

- loops (while and for);

- subprograms;

- saving to and reading from a .csv file.

The Challenge

You need to create a program that will store the user ID and passwords for the users of a system. It should display the following menu:

```
1) Create a new User ID
2) Change a password
3) Display all User IDs
4) Quit

Enter Selection:
```

If the user selects 1, it should ask them to enter a user ID. It should check if the user ID is already in the list. If it is, the program should display a suitable message and ask them to select another user ID. Once a suitable user ID has been entered it should ask for a password. Passwords should be scored with 1 point for each of the following:

- it should have at least 8 characters;

- it should include uppercase letters;

- it should include lower case letters;

- it should include numbers; and

- it should include at least one special character such as !, £, $, %, &, <, * or @.

If the password scores only 1 or 2 it should be rejected with a message saying it is a weak password; if it scores 3 or 4 tell them that "This password could be improved." Ask them if they want to try again. If it scores 5 tell them they have selected a strong password. Only acceptable user IDs and passwords should be added to the end of the .csv file.

If they select 2 from the menu they will need to enter a user ID, check to see if the user ID exists in the list, and if it does, allow the user to change the password and save the changes to the .csv file. Make sure the program only alters the existing password and does not create a new record.

If the user selects 3 from the menu, display all the user IDs but not the passwords.

If the user selects 4 from the menu it should stop the program.

Problems You Will Have to Overcome

As existing data in .csv files cannot be edited and can only be read or added to, you will need to import the data as a temporary list into Python so you can make the changes before the data is written to the .csv file afresh.

Make sure only passwords belonging to an existing user ID can be altered.

Use suitable messages to guide the user easily through the system.

Repeat the menu until they quit the program.

Answer

For this challenge you will need to set up a .csv file first, called "passwords.csv". You can either use code to do this or simply create an Excel file and save it as a .csv file. It needs to be stored in the same location as the file.

```python
import csv

def get_data():
    file = list(csv.reader(open("passwords.csv")))
    tmp = []
    for x in file:
        tmp.append(x)
    return tmp


def create_userID(tmp):
    name_again = True
    while name_again == True:
        userID = input("Enter a new user ID: ")
        userID.lower()
        inlist = False
        row = 0
        for y in tmp:
            if userID in tmp[row][0]:
                print(userID,"has already been allocated")
                inlist = True
            row = row + 1
        if inlist == False:
            name_again = False
    return userID
```

Continues on next page...

```
def create_password():
    sclist = ["!","£","$","%","^","&","*","(",")","?","@","#"]
    nclist = ["1","2","3","4","5","6","7","8","9","0"]
    tryagain = True
    while tryagain == True:
        score = 0
        uc = False
        lc = False
        sc = False
        nc = False
        password = input("Enter Password: ")
        length = len(password)
        if length >= 8:
            score = score + 1
        for x in password:
            if x.islower():
                lc = True
            if x.isupper():
                uc = True
            if x in sclist:
                sc = True
            if x in nclist:
                nc = True
        if sc == True:
            score = score + 1
        if lc == True:
            score = score + 1
        if uc == True:
            score = score + 1
        if nc == True:
            score = score + 1
        if score == 1 or score == 2:
            print("This is a week password, try again")
        if score == 3 or score == 4:
            print("This password could be imporved")
            again = input("Do you want to try for a stronger password? (y/n) ")
            again.lower()
            if again == "n":
                tryagain = False
        if password != password2:
            print("Passwords do not match.  File not saved")
            main()
        else:
            return password
```

Continues on next page...

```
def find_userID(tmp):
    ask_name_again = True
    userID = ""
    while ask_name_again == True:
        searchID = input("Enter the user ID you are looking for ")
        searchID.lower()
        inlist = False
        row = 0
        for y in tmp:
            if searchID in tmp[row][0]:
                inlist = True
            row = row + 1
        if inlist == True:
            userID = searchID
            ask_name_again = False
        else:
            print(searchID,"is NOT in the list")
    return userID

def change_password(userID,tmp):
    if userID != "":
        password = create_password()
        ID = userID.index(userID)
        tmp[ID][1] = password
        file = open("passwords.csv","w")
        x = 0
        for row in tmp:
            newrecord = tmp[x][0] + ", " + tmp[x][1] + "\n"
            file.write(newrecord)
            x = x + 1
        file.close()

def display_all_userID():
    tmp = get_data()
    x = 0
    for row in tmp:
        print(tmp[x][0])
        x = x + 1


def main():
    tmp = get_data()
    go_again = True
    while go_again == True:
        print()
        print("1) Create a new User ID")
        print("2) Change a password")
        print("3) Display all User IDs")
        print("4) Quit")
        print()
        selection = int(input("Enter Selection: "))
        if selection == 1:
            userID = create_userID(tmp)
            password = create_password()
            file = open("passwords.csv","a")
            newrecord = userID + ", " + password + "\n"
            file.write(str(newrecord))
            file.close()
        elif selection == 2:
            userID = find_userID(tmp)
            change_password(userID,tmp)
        elif selection == 3:
            display_all_userID()
        elif selection == 4:
            go_again = False
        else:
            print("Incorrect selection")

main()
```

149: Times Tables (GUI)

In this challenge you will need to use the following skills:

- loops (while and for);
- subprograms;
- Tkinter library.

The Challenge

Create a program that will display the following screen:

When the user enters a number in the first box and clicks on the "View Times Table" button it should show the times table in the list area.

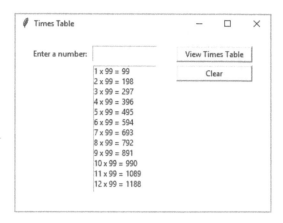

For instance, if the user entered 99 they would see the list as shown in the example on the right.

The "Clear" button should clear both boxes.

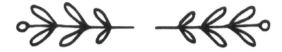

Problems You
Will Have to Overcome

You want to display the number sentence in the list rather than just the answers. The following line of code may help you do this:

```
num_list.insert(END,(i, "x", num, "=", answer))
```

Make sure it is as easy to use as possible by making sure the focus is in the correct location.

Answer

```python
from tkinter import *

def show_table():
    num = num_box.get()
    num = int(num)
    value = 1
    for i in range(1, 13):
        answer = i * num
        num_list.insert(END,(i, "x", num, "=", answer))
        value = value + 1
    num_box.delete(0, END)
    num_box.focus()

def clear_list():
    num_box.delete(0, END)
    num_list.delete(0, END)
    num_box.focus()

window = Tk()
window.title("Times Table")
window.geometry("400x280")


label1 = Label(text = "Enter a number:")
label1.place(x = 20, y = 20, width = 100, height = 25)

num_box = Entry(text = 0)
num_box.place(x = 120, y = 20, width = 100, height = 25)
num_box.focus()

button1 = Button(text = "View Times Table", command = show_table)
button1.place(x = 250, y = 20, width = 120, height = 25)

num_list = Listbox()
num_list.place(x = 120, y = 50, width = 100, height = 200)

button2 = Button(text = "Clear", command = clear_list)
button2.place(x = 250, y = 50, width = 120, height = 25)

window.mainloop()
```

150: Art Gallery

In this challenge you will need to use the following skills:

- Tkinter library;

- SQLite 3.

The Challenge

A small art gallery is selling works from different artists and wants to keep track of the paintings using an SQL database. You need to create a user-friendly system to keep track of the art. This should include using a GUI. Below is the current data that needs to be stored in a database.

Artists Contact Details:

ArtistID	Name	Address	Town	County	Postcode
1	Martin Leighton	5 Park Place	Peterborough	Cambridgeshire	PE32 5LP
2	Eva Czarniecka	77 Warner Close	Chelmsford	Essex	CM22 5FT
3	Roxy Parkin	90 Hindhead Road		London	SE12 6WM
4	Nigel Farnworth	41 Whitby Road	Huntly	Aberdeenshire	AB54 5PN
5	Teresa Tanner	70 Guild Street		London	NW7 1SP

Pieces of Art:

PieceID	ArtistID	Title	Medium	Price
1	5	Woman with black Labrador	Oil	220
2	5	Bees & thistles	Watercolour	85
3	2	A stroll to Westminster	Ink	190
4	1	African giant	Oil	800
5	3	Water daemon	Acrylic	1700
6	4	A seagull	Watercolour	35
7	1	Three friends	Oil	1800
8	2	Summer breeze 1	Acrylic	1350
9	4	Mr Hamster	Watercolour	35
10	1	Pulpit Rock, Dorset	Oil	600
11	5	Trawler Dungeness beach	Oil	195
12	2	Dance in the snow	Oil	250
13	4	St Tropez port	Ink	45
14	3	Pirate assassin	Acrylic	420
15	1	Morning walk	Oil	800
16	4	A baby barn swallow	Watercolour	35
17	4	The old working mills	Ink	395

Problems You Will Have to Overcome

The art gallery must be able to add new artists and pieces of art.

Once a piece of art has been sold, the data about that art should be removed from the main SQL database and stored in a separate text file.

Users should be able to search by artist, medium or price.

Answer

```python
import sqlite3
from tkinter import *

def addartist():
    newname = artistname.get()
    newaddress = artistadd.get()
    newtown = artisttown.get()
    newcounty = artistcounty.get()
    newpostcode = artistpostcode.get()
    cursor.execute("""INSERT INTO Artists (name,address,town,county,postcode)
VALUES (?,?,?,?,?)""",(newname,newaddress,newtown,newcounty,newpostcode))
    db.commit()
    artistname.delete(0,END)
    artistadd.delete(0,END)
    artisttown.delete(0,END)
    artistcounty.delete(0,END)
    artistpostcode.delete(0,END)
    artistname.focus()

def clearartist():
    artistname.delete(0,END)
    artistadd.delete(0,END)
    artisttown.delete(0,END)
    artistcounty.delete(0,END)
    artistpostcode.delete(0,END)
    artistname.focus()

def addart():
    newartname = artname.get()
    newtitle = arttitle.get()
    newmedium = medium.get()
    newprice = artprice.get()
    cursor.execute("""INSERT INTO Art (artistid,title,medium,price)
VALUES (?,?,?,?)""",(newartname,newtitle,newmedium,newprice))
    db.commit()
    artname.delete(0,END)
    arttitle.delete(0,END)
    medium.set("")
    artprice.delete(0,END)
    artistname.focus()

def clearwindow():
    outputwindow.delete(0,END)

def viewartists():
    cursor.execute("SELECT * FROM Artists")
    for x in cursor.fetchall():
        newrecord = str(x[0]) + ",   " + str(x[1]) + ", " + str(x[2]) + ", "+ str(x[3]) + ", " + str(x[4]) + ", " + x[5] + "\n"
        outputwindow.insert(END,newrecord)

def viewart():
    cursor.execute("SELECT * FROM Art")
    for x in cursor.fetchall():
        newrecord = str(x[0]) + ",   " + str(x[1]) + ",   " + str(x[2]) + ", " + str(x[3]) + ",    £" + str(x[4]) + "\n"
        outputwindow.insert(END,newrecord)

def searchartistoutput():
    selectedartist = searchartist.get()
    cursor.execute("SELECT name FROM Artists WHERE artistid=?",[selectedartist])
    for x in cursor.fetchall():
        outputwindow.insert(END,x)
        cursor.execute("SELECT * FROM Art WHERE artistid=?",[selectedartist])
        for x in cursor.fetchall():
            newrecord = str(x[0]) + ",   " + str(x[1]) + ",   "+str(x[2]) + ",    " + str(x[3]) + ",    £" + str(x[4]) + "\n"
            outputwindow.insert(END,newrecord)
    searchartist.delete(0,END)
    searchartist.focus()
```

Continues on next page…

```
def searchmediumoutput():
    selectedmedium = medium2.get()
    cursor.execute("""SELECT Art.pieceid, Artists.name, Art.title, Art.medium, Art.price
FROM Artists,Art WHERE Artists.artistid=Art.artistid AND Art.medium=?""",[selectedmedium])
    for x in cursor.fetchall():
        newrecord = str(x[0]) + ",   " + str(x[1]) + ",   " + str(x[2]) + ",   " + str(x[3]) + ",   £" + str(x[4]) + "\n"
        outputwindow.insert(END,newrecord)
    medium2.set("")

def searchbyprice():
    minprice = selectmin.get()
    maxprice = selectmax.get()
    cursor.execute("""SELECT Art.pieceid, Artists.name, Art.title, Art.medium, Art.price
FROM Artists,Art WHERE Artists.artistid=Art.artistid AND Art.price>=? AND Art.price<=?""",[minprice,maxprice])
    for x in cursor.fetchall():
        newrecord = str(x[0]) + ",   " + str(x[1]) + ",   " + str(x[2]) + ",   " + str(x[3]) + ",   £" + str(x[4]) + "\n"
        outputwindow.insert(END,newrecord)
    selectmin.delete(0,END)
    selectmax.delete(0,END)
    selectmin.focus()

def sold():
    file = open("SoldArt.txt","a")
    selectedpiece = soldpiece.get()
    cursor.execute("SELECT * FROM Art WHERE pieceid=?",[selectedpiece])
    for x in cursor.fetchall():
        newrecord = str(x[0]) + ", " + str(x[1]) + ", " + str(x[2]) + ", " + str(x[3]) + ", "+str(x[4]) + "\n"
        file.write(newrecord)
    file.close()
    cursor.execute("DELETE FROM Art WHERE pieceid=?",[selectedpiece])
    db.commit()


with sqlite3.connect("Art.db") as db:
    cursor = db.cursor()

cursor.execute(""" CREATE TABLE IF NOT EXISTS Artists(
artistid integer PRIMARY KEY, name text, address text, town text, county text, postcode text); """)

cursor.execute(""" CREATE TABLE IF NOT EXISTS Art(
pieceid integer PRIMARY KEY, artistid integer, title text, medium text, price integer); """)

window = Tk()
window.title("Art")
window.geometry("1220x600")

title1 = Label(text = "Enter new details:")
title1.place(x = 10, y = 10,width = 100, height = 25)
artistnamelbl = Label(text = "Name:")
artistnamelbl.place(x = 30, y = 40,width = 80, height = 25)
artistname = Entry(text = "")
artistname.place(x = 110, y = 40, width = 200, height = 25)
artistname.focus()
artistaddlbl = Label(text = "Address:")
artistaddlbl.place(x = 310, y = 40,width = 80, height = 25)
artistadd = Entry(text = "")
artistadd.place(x = 390, y = 40, width = 200, height = 25)
artisttownlbl = Label(text = "Town:")
artisttownlbl.place(x = 590, y = 40,width = 80, height = 25)
artisttown = Entry(text = "")
artisttown.place(x = 670, y = 40, width = 100, height = 25)
artistcountylbl = Label(text = "County:")
artistcountylbl.place(x = 770, y = 40,width = 80, height = 25)
artistcounty = Entry(text = "")
artistcounty.place(x = 850, y = 40, width = 100, height = 25)
artistpostcodelbl = Label(text = "Postcode:")
artistpostcodelbl.place(x = 950, y = 40,width = 80, height = 25)
artistpostcode = Entry(text = "")
artistpostcode.place(x = 1030, y = 40, width = 100, height = 25)
addbtn = Button(text = "Add Artist", command = addartist)
addbtn.place(x = 110, y = 80, width = 130, height = 25)
clearbtn = Button(text = "Clear Artist", command = clearartist)
clearbtn.place(x = 250, y = 80, width = 130, height = 25)
```

Continues on next page...

```
artnamelbl = Label(text = "Artist ID:")
artnamelbl.place(x = 30, y = 120,width = 80, height = 25)
artname = Entry(text = "")
artname.place(x = 110, y = 120, width = 50, height = 25)
arttitlelbl = Label(text = "Title:")
arttitlelbl.place(x = 200, y = 120,width = 80, height = 25)
arttitle = Entry(text = "")
arttitle.place(x = 280, y = 120, width = 280, height = 25)
artmediumlbl = Label(text = "Medium:")
artmediumlbl.place(x = 590, y = 120,width = 80, height = 25)
medium = StringVar(window)
artmedium = OptionMenu(window, medium, "Oil","Watercolour", "Ink", "Acrylic")
artmedium.place(x = 670, y = 120, width = 100, height = 25)
artpricelbl = Label(text = "Price:")
artpricelbl.place(x = 770, y = 120,width = 80, height = 25)
artprice = Entry(text = "")
artprice.place(x = 850, y = 120, width = 100, height = 25)
addartbtn = Button(text = "Add Piece", command = addart)
addartbtn.place(x = 110, y = 150, width = 130, height = 25)
clearartbtn = Button(text = "Clear Piece", command = clearart)
clearartbtn.place(x = 250, y = 150, width = 130, height = 25)

outputwindow = Listbox()
outputwindow.place(x = 10,y = 200, width = 1000, height = 350)

clearoutputwindow = Button(text = "Clear Output", command = clearwindow)
clearoutputwindow.place(x = 1020, y = 200, width = 155, height = 25)
viewallartists = Button(text = "View All Artists", command = viewartists)
viewallartists.place(x = 1020, y = 230, width = 155, height = 25)
viewallart = Button(text = "View All Art", command = viewart)
viewallart.place(x = 1020, y = 260, width = 155, height = 25)
searchartist = Entry(text = "")
searchartist.place(x = 1020, y = 300, width = 50, height = 25)
searchartistbtn = Button(text = "Search by Artist", command = searchartistoutput)
searchartistbtn.place(x = 1075, y = 300, width = 100, height = 25)
medium2 = StringVar(window)
searchmedium = OptionMenu(window, medium2, "Oil","Watercolour", "Ink", "Acrylic")
searchmedium.place(x = 1020, y = 330, width = 100, height = 25)
searchmediumbtn = Button(text = "Search", command = searchmediumoutput)
searchmediumbtn.place(x = 1125, y = 330, width = 50, height = 25)
minlbl = Label(text = "Min:")
minlbl.place(x = 1020, y = 360,width = 75, height = 25)
maxlbl = Label(text = "Max:")
maxlbl.place(x = 1100, y = 360,width = 75, height = 25)
selectmin = Entry(text = "")
selectmin.place(x = 1020, y = 380, width = 75, height = 25)
selectmax = Entry(text = "")
selectmax.place(x = 1100, y = 380, width=75, height=25)
searchpricebtn = Button(text = "Search by Price", command = searchbyprice)
searchpricebtn.place(x = 1020, y = 410, width = 155, height = 25)
soldpiece = Entry(text = "")
soldpiece.place(x = 1020, y = 450, width = 50, height = 25)
soldbtn = Button(text = "Sold", command = sold)
soldbtn.place(x = 1075, y = 450, width = 100, height = 25)

window.mainloop()
db.close()
```

What Next?

If you have worked through all the examples in this book you should have a good understanding of the basics of programming with Python. You will have become familiar with the syntax of the language and started to think like a programmer by breaking down larger problems into small, manageable chunks you know how to solve. You should look back on all you have learnt and can justifiably feel a smirk of satisfaction at what you have achieved. Learning to program takes dedication and you have shown you can persevere, and you now have the basic skills to continue on your journey into Python.

The skills you have learnt in this book will allow you to create powerful programs, but now is not the time to sit back and relax. You need to go out into the big programming world and find out how other programmers work. Search the internet, find new challenges. As you explore you will see code that is unfamiliar to you as there are several variations that can be used. For instance, with Tkinter there is another method called "pack" which many programmers prefer. It allows you to use a grid method for designing your screens but does not allow you to fine-tune the position of an object the way the place method we have been using allows. Try it out, you may prefer it, but do be careful as some techniques do not work well with others. If you want to use the pack method then please don't try to mix it with the place method in the same program. Python doesn't like working with two different systems simultaneously and will crash.

The best way to learn more advanced programming techniques is to try them out. Look at other people's code and visit some chat forums. Programmers are very helpful and as long as you are not asking a question that has already been answered on the forum they are generally willing to help you out. If you are stuck on a piece of code, then ask for help in a forum; programmers like nothing more than to solve a problem. You may not necessarily agree with their solution, it may not be the method you are looking to use, but it will give you an idea of how to look at it with fresh eyes and can show you a route to a possible solution you had not considered before.

Whether you feel satisfied with your knowledge or want to explore further, I hope you have enjoyed your venture into programming and this book has proved useful.

Glossary

Term	Description
2D list	Creates a multi-dimensional list. For instance, to create the following table of data: |	0	1	2 | |---|---|---|---| | 0 | 23 | 16 | 34 | | 1 | 45 | 29 | 48 | enter the following code: `number_list = [[23,16,34],[45,29,48]]`

addition	Adds two values together if they are numbers
	`total = num1 + num2`
	or joins them if they contain text (see concatenation).
	`name = firstname + surname`

and	Used to specify that both conditions must be met to return a true value.
	`if num > 10 and num < 20:`
	`    print("In range")`
	`else:`
	`    print("Out of range")`

append	Adds a single item to the end of a list, tuple, dictionary, string or an array. `names_list.append("Timothy")`

append to a file	Opens an existing text or .csv file and allows data to be added to the end of the existing contents.
	`file = open("Countries.txt", "a")`
	`file.write("France\n")`
	`file.close`
	See also write to a file, write to non-existing file, read a file

argument	A value passed to a subprogram. In this example UserAns is the argument and would have been defined outside of the subprogram.
	`def CheckAnswer(UserAns):`
	`    if UserAns == 20:`
	`        print("Correct")`
	`    else:`
	`        print("Wrong")`

array	In Python arrays are similar to lists but they are only used to store numbers. The user defines the specific number type, i.e. integer, long, double or floating-point.
	`nums = array('i',[45,324,654,45,264])`
	`print(nums)`
	If the array needs to store strings a list is required.

blob	A data type that is stored exactly as it was input. See SQL and database.

Term	Description

button	Used in a GUI with Tkinter. The code below creates a button that will run the subprogram "click".
	``python
	button1 = Button(text = "Click here", command = click)
	``
	See Tkinter.

capitalize	Changes the case so the first letter is uppercase and all other letters are lower case.
	``python
	print(name.capitalize())
	``

choice	Selects a random choice from a list of options.
	``python
	selection = random.choice(['a','b','c'])
	``

comma-separated values	A common textual representation for tables in which the values in each row are separated by commas. See csv.

comments	Used to explain how a program works or to block out pieces of code for testing other sections. Starts with the # symbol.
	``python
	if salary > 50000: #This is a comment
	    print("Too high")
	
	#This is another comment
	``

compiler	Translates a program written in a high-level language such as Python into a low-level language such as machine code.

concatenation	Joins two strings together to form one string (see addition).
	``python
	name = firstname + surname
	``

conditional statement	Statement used to test out a condition. Commonly used in if statements, while and for loops.
	``python
	if guess == num:
	``

count	Counts the number of times a piece of data appears in a list, tuple, dictionary, string or an array.
	``python
	print(names_list.count("Sue"))
	``

csv	A file type, similar to a spreadsheet or database, where data is stored in rows and columns. See comma-separated values.

curly brackets	Defines the values inside a dictionary.
	``python
	scores = {"Tim":20,"Sue":35,"Bob":29}
	``

database	A structured set of data. The data is held in tables and these are made up of fields and records. See SQL, tables, fields and records.
debugging	The process of finding and removing programming errors.
decimal point	See floating-point number.

def	Defines a subprogram.
	``python
	def menu():
	    print("1) Open")
	    print("2) Close")
	    selection = int(input("Selection: "))
	``

defining a subprogram	Creates a subprogram so that it can be used in other parts of the program. See def.

del	Deletes an item from a list. For example:
	``python
	del names_list[2]
	``
	Deletes item 2 from the "names_list".

dictionary	A type of list in which user-defined indexes are mapped to values.
	``python
	scores = {"Tim":20,"Sue":35,"Bob":29}
	``

division	Divides one value by another and displays the answer as a floating-point number.
	``python
	>>> 5/2
	2.5
	``

Term	Description
double	Allows decimal places with numbers ranging from minus 10,308 to 10,308.
drop-down menu	See option menu and Tkinter.
| elif | Used in an if statement to check a new condition if previous conditions have not been met.<br><br>```python
if num < 10:
    print("Too low")
elif num > 20:
    print("Too high")
else:
    print("In range")
``` |
| else | Used in an if statement to define what happens if the previous conditions have not been met.<br><br>```python
if num < 10:
    print("Too low")
elif num > 20:
    print("Too high")
else:
    print("In range")
``` |
| else...if | See elif. |
| entry box | Used in a GUI with Tkinter to allow the user to input data or used to display output. The code below creates a blank entry box.<br><br>```python
entry_box = Entry(text = 0)
```<br>See Tkinter. |
| equal to | The double equal symbol is used to compare values<br><br>```python
if guess == num:
``` |
| extend | Adds multiple items to the end of a list, tuple, dictionary, string or an array.<br><br>```python
names_list.extend(more_names)
``` |
| field | In a database a field is a single piece of data such as a name, date of birth or telephone number that is stored in a table. See SQL, database, table and record. |
| floating-point number | Allows decimal places with numbers ranging from minus 1,038 to 1,038 (i.e. allows up to 38 numeric characters including a single decimal point anywhere in that number and can be negative or positive value)<br><br>```python
num = float(input("Enter number: "))
``` |
| for loop | A type of loop which will repeat the block of code a set number of times.<br><br>```python
for i in range(1,5):
    print(i)
``` |
| forward | Moves the turtle forward; if the pen is down this will leave a trail behind it as it moves, drawing a straight line on the screen.<br><br>```python
turtle.forward(50)
```<br>In the above example it will move 50 steps. |
| greater than | To check if one value is larger than another.<br><br>```python
num1 > num2
``` |
| greater than or equal to | To check if one value is larger than or equal to another.<br><br>```python
num1 >= num2
``` |
| GUI | GUI stands for graphical user interface and uses windows, entry boxes and menus, which can be manipulated by a mouse. See Tkinter. |

Term	Description
hash	See comments.
IDLE	Stands for "integrated development environment" and is a basic editor and interpreter environment for Python.
| if statement | Checks to see if a condition is met; if it is it will perform the subsequent lines of code.<br><br>```
if num < 100:
    print("too low")
``` |
| images | Images can be displayed using GUI. There are two ways images can be seen. In this first block of code the logo will be shown and this will not change as the program is running.<br><br>```
logo = PhotoImage(file = "logo.gif")
logoimage = Label(image = logo)
logoimage.place(x = 30, y = 20, width = 200, height = 120)
```<br><br>In this second block of code the image will change depending on the value selected in an option menu.<br><br>```
photo = PhotoImage(file = "logo.gif")
photobox = Label(window, image = photo)
photobox.image = photo
photobox.place(x = 200, y = 200, width = 200, height = 120)
```<br><br>See Tkinter and option menu. |
| immutable | Unchangeable. The value of immutable data cannot be altered after it has been created, e.g. the data in a tuple is immutable and therefore once a program starts running it cannot be changed. |
| in | Can be used to check a character is in a string. This is useful in both for and if statements. This is an example of a for statement which will print each character on a separate line:<br><br>```
for i in msg:
    print(i)
```<br><br>Here is an example to see if a letter is within a string:<br><br>```
msg = input("Enter text: ")
letter = input("Enter letter: ")
if letter in msg:
    print("Thank you")
else:
    print("Not in string")
``` |
| indent | Used in Python to denote lines that belong to another statement. For instance, in a for loop the lines beneath it are indented as they are within the loop, the lines that are not indented are outside the loop.<br><br>```
for n in range(0,10):
    count = n + 1
    print (count)
print("The end")
```<br><br>To indent a line, you can hit either the tab key or use the space bar. |
| index | A number that specifies the location of a single value in a list, tuple, dictionary or string. Python starts counting from 0, not 1, so if the index is automatically generated the first item would have the index value of 0.<br><br>```
colours = ["red","blue","green"]
print(colours.index("blue"))
``` |
| indices | The double * is used to represent "to the power of" i.e. 4**2 is 42. |
```

Term	Description
input	Allows the user to input a value. This is usually assigned to a variable name. `name = input("Enter name: ")`
insert	Inserts an item into a set position in the list and pushes everything else along to make space. This will change their index numbers according to their new position in the list. `names_list.insert(1,"Gary")`
int	Used to define a number as an integer. `num = int(input("Enter number: "))`
integer	A whole number between minus 32,768 and 32,767.
interpret	To execute a program by translating it one line at a time.

islower	Used to check if a string contains only lower case letters.
	`if msg.islower():`
	`    print("This message is in lowercase")`

isupper	Used to check if a string contains only upper case letters.
	`if msg.isupper():`
	`    print("This message is in uppercase")`

iteration	Repeating code, for instance in a for or a while loop.
label	Used in a GUI with Tkinter to display text of an image. The code below creates a label on the screen displaying the message shown. `label1 = Label(text = "Enter a number:")` See Tkinter.
left	Turns the turtle counter clockwise. `turtle.left(120)` In the above example it will turn 120°.
len	Determines the length of the variable. `print(len(name))`
less than	To check if one value is smaller than another. `num1 < num2`
less than or equal to	To check if one value is smaller than or equal to another. `num1 <= num2`

library	A collection of code that can be used to perform a specific function. This is code that is not in Python standard blocks of code but can be imported as needed. To do this, import the library at the beginning of the program.
	`import math`
	`radius = int(input("Enter the radius: "))`
	`r2 = radius**2`
	`area = math.pi*r2`
	`print(area)`

line break	Forces the text onto a new line.
	`print("Hello\nHow are you?")`
	Produces the output:
	`Hello`
	`How are you?`

list	Used like an array in other programming languages. Lists allow a group of data to be stored under a single variable name and can be altered while the program is running.
	`list=['a','b','c']`
	`for i in list:`
	`    print(i)`

Term	Description
list box	Used in a GUI with Tkinter. The code below creates a list box that is only used for output. `list_box = Listbox()` See Tkinter.
logic errors	An error that is tricky to spot. The program may look like it works (i.e. no error message appears) but the theory behind the program is incorrect so it is not working correctly. For instance, when the wrong comparison symbol is used.
long	Whole number between minus 2,147,483,648 and 2,147,483,647.
loop	See for loop and while loop.
lower case	Changes a string to lower case. `name = name.lower()`

multiplication	Multiplies two values together.
	
	`>>> 3*4`
	`12`

nested	A sequence inside another sequence, for instance a for loop may be inside an if statement and therefore the for loop is known as a nested statement inside the if statement.
	
	`if num < 20:`
	`    for i in range(1,num):`
	`        print (i)`
	`    else:`
	`        print("Too high")`

not equal to	Used to check if two values are not equal. `num1 != num2`

not null	When creating an SQL table, you can specify if a field is not allowed to be left blank when a new record is created.
	
	`cursor.execute(""" CREATE TABLE IF NOT EXISTS employees(`
	`id integer PRIMARY KEY,`
	`name text NOT NULL,`
	`dept text NOT NULL,`
	`salary integer); """)`
	
	See SQL, database, table and field.

option menu	Creates a drop-down menu in a GUI.
	
	`selectname = StringVar(window)`
	`selectname.set("Select Name")`
	
	`nameslist = OptionMenu(window, selectname, "Bob","Sue","Tim")`
	`nameslist.place(x = 30, y = 250)`
	
	See Tkinter.

or	Used to specify that only one condition needs to be met.
	
	`if choice == "a" or choice == "b":`
	`    print("Thank you")`
	`else:`
	`    print("Incorrect selection")`

output box	Used in a GUI with Tkinter and creates a message box which is used to display output. `output_box = Message(text = 0)` See Tkinter.
passing variables	Creating or altering a variable in one subprogram and allowing it to be used in another section of the program. See subprogram.
pendown	Places the pen on the page so that when the turtle moves it will leave a trail behind it. By default, the pen is down. `turtle.pendown()`

Term	Description
penup	Removes the pen from the page so that as the turtle moves it does not leave a trail behind it. `turtle.penup()`

pi	Gives pi (π) to 15 decimal places.
	
	```import math```
	```radius = int(input("Enter the radius: "))```
	```r2 = radius**2```
	```area = math.pi*r2```
	```print(area)```

pop	Removes the last item from a list, tuple, dictionary, string or an array. `names_list.pop()`
power of	See indices.

primary key	A primary key in a database is a unique identifying field for each record.
	
	```cursor.execute(""" CREATE TABLE IF NOT EXISTS employees(```
	``` id integer PRIMARY KEY,```
	``` name text NOT NULL,```
	``` dept text NOT NULL,```
	``` salary integer); """)```
	
	See SQL, database, table, record and field.

print	Displays the contents between the brackets on screen. `print("Hello", name)`
prompt	Shown as >>> in the Python shell window and allows the user to input directly into the shell.

query	A query is used to extract data from the database.
	
	```cursor.execute("""SELECT employees.id,employees.name,dept.manager```
	``` FROM employees,dept WHERE employees.dept=dept.dept```
	``` AND employees.dept='Sales'""")```
	```for x in cursor.fetchall():```
	``` print(x)```
	
	See SQL, database, table and field.

quote mark	See speech mark.
randint	Generates a random number. `num = random.randint(1,10)`
random	Generates a random floating point number between 0 and 1. `num = random.random()`

random library	To use the random library in Python you must have the line "import random" at the start of your program. See also randint, choice, random and randrange.
	
	```import random```
	```num = random.randint(1,10)```
	```correct = False```
	```while correct == False:```
	``` guess = int(input("Enter a number: "))```
	``` if guess == num:```
	``` correct = True```
	``` elif guess > num:```
	``` print("Too high")```
	``` else:```
	``` print("Too low")```

randrange	Picks a number from within a range of numbers. It is possible to even select the steps that range can take, for instance: `num = random.randrange(0,100,5)` This will pick a random number between the numbers 0 and 100 in steps of 5, e.g. it will only pick from 0, 5, 10, 15, 20, etc.

Term	Description

range	Used to define a starting and end number in a range and can include the step (the difference between each number in the sequence). Usually used as part of a for loop.
	
	```for i in range(1,10,2):```
	``` print (i)```
	
	Would produce the output:
	
	```>>>```
	```1```
	```3```
	```5```
	```7```
	```9```

read a file	Opens an existing text or .csv file so the data can be read.
	
	```file = open("Countries.txt", "r")```
	```print (file.read())```
	
	See also write to a file, write to non-existing file, append to a file

real	A data type used in SQL databases that can store a decimal place. See floating-point number, SQL and database.
record	In a database a record is one complete set of fields; for example one employee's set of data would be stored in a single row of a table. See SQL, database, table and field.

remainder	Finds the remainder after a whole number division.
	
	```>>> 5%2```
	```1```

remove	Deletes an item from the list. This is useful if you do not know the index of that item. If there is more than one instance of the data it will only delete the first instance of that data. ```names_list.remove("Tom")```
reverse	Reverses the order of a list, tuple, dictionary, string or an array. ```names_list.reverse()```
right	Turns the turtle clockwise. ```turtle.right(90)``` In the above example it will turn 90°.
round	Rounds a variable to a specified number of decimal places. ```newnum = round(num,2)```

round brackets	Defines the values inside the brackets as a tuple. See tuple.
	
	```tuple =('a','b','c')```
	```for i in tuple:```
	``` print(i)```

run time error	These errors only crop up when you try to run the program. For instance, it may not be able to work with a variable as it is saved as a string when it is expecting an integer. Run time errors will crash the program and display an error message such as the following.
	
	```Traceback (most recent call last):```
	``` File "C:/Python34/CHALLENGES/testingagain.py", line 2, in <module>```
	``` total = num + 100```
	```TypeError: Can't convert 'int' object to str implicitly```

running a program	Select the Run menu and select Run Module, alternatively use the F5 key. The program must be saved before it can run.
shell	The first screen you see when you launch Python.

Term	Description
sort	Sorts a list into alphabetical order and saves the list in the new order. This does not work if the list is storing data of different types, such as strings and numeric data in the same list. `names_list.sort()`
sorted	Prints a list in alphabetical order. This does not alter the order of the original list and it is still kept in the original order. This does not work if the list is storing data of different types, such as strings and numeric data in the same list. `print(sorted(names_list))`
space (removal)	See strip.

speech marks	Used to define a block of code as a string. You can use either double quotes (") or single quotes (') but whatever you use to start your string you must use the same style to define the end of the string.
	
	 `print("This is a string")`
	
	 You can use triple speech marks to preserve the formatting such as line breaks.
	
	 `address="""123 Long Lane`
	 `Oldtown`
	 `AB1 23CD"""`
	 `print(address)`

SQL	Stands for Structured Query Language, which is used to communicate with a database. A database can contain several tables joined together, which is known as a relation database. Each table is made up of fields that contain similar data such as ID, Name, Address, etc. Each row in the table is known as a record. See database, field, record, table and query.
SQLite	A simple database that is free to download and works well with Python.

sqrt	Works out the square root of a number. You need to import the math library at the start of your program for this to work.
	
	 `import math`
	 `num = math.sqrt(100)`
	 `print(num)`

square brackets	Defines the values inside the brackets as a list. See list.
	
	 `list=['a','b','c']`
	 `for i in list:`
	 `    print(i)`

square root	See sqrt.
str	A data type as string. See string. `year = str(year)`
string	Can include letters, numbers and various symbols and be enclosed by either double or single quotes. They cannot be used in a calculation, even if they only contain numbers. They can, however, be used in concatenation and joined onto other strings to make a larger string. See concatenation.

strip	Removes additional characters from the start and end of a string.
	
	 `text = "   This is some text.   "`
	 `print(text.strip(" "))`

Structured Query Language	See SQL.

Term	Description

subprogram	A block of code that can be called to run from another section of the program and can return a value.
	
	``python
	def get_data():
	    user_name = input("Enter your name: ")
	    user_age = int(input("Enter age: "))
	    data_tuple = (user_name, user_age)
	    return data_tuple
	
	def message(user_name, user_age):
	    if user_age <= 10:
	        print("Hi", user_name)
	    else:
	        print("Hello", user_name)
	
	def main():
	    user_name,user_age = get_data()
	    message(user_name, user_age)
	
	main()
	``

subtraction	Subtracts one value from another.
	
	``
	>>> 5-2
	3
	``

syntax error	A programming error that occurs when statements are in the wrong order or contain typographical errors.
table	A container for the data. A database may contain more than one table and these can be linked together. Below is an example of a table to store employees' data. Table: Employees |	ID	Name	Dept	Salary
---	---	---	---	---
	Filter	Filter	Filter	Filter
1	1	Bob	Sales	25000
2	2	Sue	IT	28500
3	3	Tim	Sales	25000
4	4	Anne	Admin	18500
5	5	Paul	IT	28500
6	6	Simon	Sales	22000
7	7	Karen	Manufacturing	18500
8	8	Mark	Manufacturing	19000
9	9	George	Manufacturing	18500
10	10	Keith	Manufacturing	15000	 See SQL, database, field and record.

Term	Description
text file	A file object that is imported into Python and allows the program to read and write string objects to that file. ``` file = open("Names.txt", "a") newname = input("Enter a new name: ") file.write(newname+"\n") file.close file = open("Names.txt", "r") print (file.read()) ```
text file	See also write to a text file, read a text file and append to a text file.
title	Changes the case so all words start with a capital and the rest are in lower case. ``` name = name.title() ```
Tkinter	Tkinter is Python's most commonly used GUI library.
to the power of	See indices.
trim spaces	See strip.
tuple	A type of list but the values cannot be altered as the program is running. Usually reserved for menu options that are unlikely to change. ``` menu =('Open','Print','Close') ```

turtle	A tool used for drawing shapes on the screen.
	
	``
	import turtle
	for i in range(0,4):
	    turtle.forward(100)
	    turtle.right(90)
	turtle.exitonclick()
	``
	
	See also forward, left, right, penup, pendown and pensize.

two-dimensional list	See 2D list.
upper	Changes a string to uppercase. ``` name = name.upper() ```
variables	Stores values such as text and numbers. The equal sign (=) is used to assign values to variables. ``` num = 54 ```

while loop	A type of loop that will repeat the block of code inside it (shown with indented rows) as long as a particular condition is being met.
	
	``
	total = 0
	while total <= 50:
	    num = int(input("Enter a number: "))
	    total = total + num
	    print("The total is...",total)
	``

whole number division	The process by which you find how many times a number (divisor) is contained in another number (dividend).
	
	``
	>>> 15//7
	2
	``

window	The screen used in a GUI. The code below creates a window, referred to as "window", adds a title and defines the size of the window. ``` window = Tk() window.title("Add title here") window.geometry("450x100") ``` See Tkinter.

Term	Description
| write to a file | Creates a new text or .csv file to save values into; if one already exists then it will be overwritten with a new file.<br><br>```
file = open("Countries.txt","w")
file.write("Italy\n")
file.write("Germany\n")
file.write("Spain\n")
file.close()
```<br>See also write to non-existing file, append to a file, read a file. |
| write to non-existing file | Creates a new file and writes to that file. If the file already exists, the program will crash rather than overwrite it.<br><br>```
file = open("newlist.csv","x")
newrecord = "Tim,43\n"
file.write(str(newrecord))
file.close()
```<br>See also write to a file, append to a file, read a file. |

Index